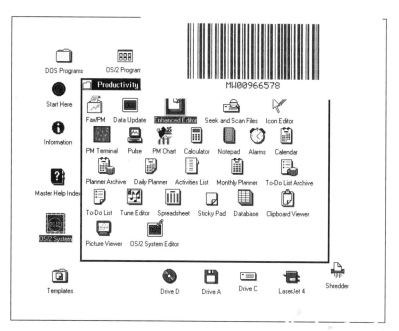

The screen image above shows the contents of the Productivity folder on the OS/2 desktop, while the table below lists all the keyboard shortcuts you can use when working with objects.

Key	Function
Arrow key	Moves between objects
Spacebar	Selects an object
Enter	Opens an object or accepts a menu selection
Esc	Closes a pop-up menu, or cancels a mouse selection
Shift+F10	Opens the selected object's pop-up menu
Home	Selects the first option in a pop-up menu
End	Selects the last option in a pop-up menu
Underlined letter	Selects a specific choice from a menu

The SYBEX Instant Reference Series

Instant References are available on these topics:

AutoCAD Release 12 for DOS

AutoCAD Release 12 for Windows

CorelDRAW 3

dBASE

dBASE IV 1.1 Programmer's

dBASE IV 2.0 Programmer's

DOS 5

DOS 6

DR DOS 6

Excel 4 for Windows

Harvard Graphics 3

Harvard Graphics for Windows

Lotus 1-2-3 Release 2.3 & 2.4 for DOS

Lotus 1-2-3 for Windows

Microsoft Access

Norton Desktop for DOS

Norton Desktop for Windows 2.0

Norton Utilities 6

Norton Utilities 7

PageMaker 4.0 for the Macintosh

Paradox 4 Programmer's

Paradox 4 User's

Paradox for Windows User's

PC Tools 7.1

PC Tools 8

Quattro Pro for Windows

Windows 3.1

Word for Windows, Version 2.0

WordPerfect 5.1 for DOS

WordPerfect 5.1 for Windows

Computer users are not all alike.
Neither are SYBEX books.

We know our customers have a variety of needs. They've told us so. And because we've listened, we've developed several distinct types of books to meet the needs of each of our customers. What are you looking for in computer help?

If you're looking for the basics, try the **ABC's** series. For a more visual approach, select full-color **Quick & Easy** books.

Running Start books are two books in one: a fast-paced tutorial, followed by a command reference.

Mastering and **Understanding** titles offer you a step-by-step introduction, plus an in-depth examination of intermediate-level features, to use as you progress.

Our **Up & Running** series is designed for computer-literate consumers who want a no-nonsense overview of new programs. Just 20 basic lessons, and you're on your way.

SYBEX **Encyclopedias**, **Desktop References**, and **A to Z** books provide a *comprehensive reference* and explanation of all of the commands, features, and functions of the subject software.

Sometimes a subject requires a special treatment that our standard series don't provide. So you'll find we have titles like **Advanced Techniques, Handbooks, Tips & Tricks,** and others that are specifically tailored to satisfy a unique need.

You'll find SYBEX publishes a variety of books on every popular software package. Looking for computer help? Help Yourself to SYBEX.

For a complete catalog of our publications:

SYBEX Inc.
2021 Challenger Drive, Alameda, CA 94501
Tel: (510) 523-8233/(800) 227-2346 Telex: 336311
SYBEX® Fax: (510) 523-2373

OS/2 2.1 Instant Reference

Peter Dyson

SYBEX®

San Francisco • Paris • Düsseldorf • Soest

Acquisitions Editor: David Clark
Developmental Editor: Gary Masters
Copy Editor: Brendan Fletcher
Project Editor: Kathleen Lattinville
Technical Editors: David Farquharson and Dan Tauber
Book Designer: Ingrid Owen
Production Artist: Alissa Feinberg
Screen Graphics: Cuong Le
Desktop Production Specialist: Thomas Goudie
Production Editor: Carolina Montilla
Proofreader: Hilda van Genderen
Indexer: Ted Laux
Cover Designer: Archer Design

Library of Congress Card Number: 92-85244
ISBN: 0-7821-1179-3

Manufactured in the United States of America
10 9 8 7 6 5 4 3 2 1

For Gene. Author! Author!

Acknowledgments

It is always a pleasure to thank the many people whose efforts make a project like this possible. I would like to express my sincere gratitude to the following people at SYBEX for their help and guidance: David Clark, Acquisitions Editor; Gary Masters, Developmental Editor; Brendan Fletcher, Copy Editor; Kathleen Lattinville, Project Editor; and David Farquharson and Dan Tauber, Technical Editors. I would also like to thank the members of the Production Department, whose hard work turns a manuscript into a book: Thomas Goudie, Typesetter; Cuong Le, Screen Graphics; Alissa Feinberg, Production Artist; Carolina Montilla, Production Editor; and Hilda van Genderen, Proofreader.

Special thanks go to Melissa Robertson, Assistant Program Manager, OS/2 2.1 Independent Vendor Marketing at IBM, for providing timely technical information.

And as always, thanks to Nancy.

Table of Contents

Part IV

Running OS/2, DOS and Windows Programs under OS/2

Part V

OS/2 Commands

Part VI

CONFIG.SYS Commands

Part VII

Batch File Commands

Index

Introduction

This book is designed for OS/2 users who want a quick, easy-to-use reference to OS/2 features and commands. It includes a description of the OS/2 graphical user interface, as well as alphabetical listings of all the commands you can use from the OS/2 command prompts, in your configuration file, or in your batch programming. Whether you are new to OS/2 or you are an old hand, you will find this book to be a convenient source of essential information about OS/2.

In many ways OS/2 represents the best of all worlds for the user, because you can run OS/2 applications, DOS applications, or Microsoft Windows applications on the same operating system, without making any changes in the way you work. You can run these programs in windows on the OS/2 desktop, or you can run them in full-screen mode if that makes more sense.

The thing to remember about the DOS and Windows environments in OS/2 is that they are actually parts of the OS/2 operating system; they are not exactly the same as the versions of MS-DOS and Windows you may have used in the past. In order to keep this distinction clear, throughout this book I will refer to Microsoft's standalone DOS as MS-DOS, and the version that you run under OS/2 as DOS. Fortunately for the OS/2 user, the differences between OS/2 DOS and MS-DOS are small, and almost always work to your advantage, giving you more options or more flexibility. The main differences between DOS 5 from Microsoft and the version of DOS you run under OS/2 are seen at the OS/2 DOS command prompt.

Table I.1 summarizes these differences by comparing the OS/2 command with the OS/2 DOS session command and the equivalent MS-DOS 5 command. The letter *a* signifies that a command is available in OS/2 or in OS/2 DOS, and it represents the standard of comparison for the other versions. If a command is identical in two separate versions, both versions will be represented by *a*.

The abbreviations used in Table I.1 are as follows:

a   Command is available.

n/a   Command is not available.

nsd   Command is not significantly different.

sd   Command is significantly different.

Table I.1: Command Comparison Chart

Command Name	OS/2	OS/2 DOS	MS-DOS
ANSI	a	n/a	n/a
APPEND	n/a	a	sd
ASSIGN	n/a	a	nsd
ATTRIB	n/a	a	nsd
BACKUP	a	n/a	nsd
BOOT	a	nsd	n/a
BREAK	a	nsd	nsd
CD (or CHDIR)	a	nsd	nsd
CHCP	a	nsd	nsd
CHKDSK	a	nsd	sd
CLS	a	nsd	nsd
CMD	a	n/a	n/a
COMMAND	n/a	a	sd
COMP	a	nsd	sd
COPY	a	nsd	sd
CREATEDD	a	n/a	n/a
DATE	a	nsd	nsd
DDINSTALL	a	n/a	n/a
DEBUG	a	nsd	nsd
DEL (or ERASE)	a	nsd	nsd
DETACH	a	n/a	n/a
DIR	a	sd	sd

Table I.1: Command Comparison Chart (continued)

Command Name	OS/2	OS/2 DOS	MS-DOS
DISKCOMP	a	nsd	sd
DISKCOPY	a	nsd	sd
DPATH	a	n/a	n/a
DOSKEY	n/a	a	nsd
EAUTIL	a	nsd	n/a
EXIT	a	nsd	nsd
FDISK	a	n/a	sd
FDISKPM	a	n/a	n/a
FIND	a	nsd	nsd
FORMAT	a	nsd	sd
FSACCESS	a	a	n/a
GRAFTABL	n/a	a	sd
HELP	a	sd	sd
JOIN	n/a	a	nsd
KEYB	a	n/a	n/a
KEYS	a	n/a	n/a
LABEL	a	nsd	nsd
MAKEINI	a	n/a	n/a
MD (or MKDIR)	a	nsd	nsd
MEM	n/a	a	a
MODE	a	sd	sd
MORE	a	nsd	nsd
MOVE	a	n/a	n/a
PATCH	a	n/a	n/a
PATH	a	nsd	nsd
PICVIEW	a	n/a	n/a
PMREXX	a	n/a	n/a
PRINT	a	sd	sd
PROMPT	a	nsd	nsd

Table I.1: Command Comparison Chart (continued)

Command Name	OS/2	OS/2 DOS	MS-DOS
PSTAT	a	n/a	n/a
RD (or RMDIR)	a	nsd	nsd
RECOVER	a	nsd	sd
REN (or RENAME)	a	nsd	nsd
REPLACE	a	nsd	nsd
RESTORE	a	n/a	nsd
SET	a	nsd	nsd
SETBOOT	a	n/a	n/a
SORT	a	nsd	nsd
SPOOL	a	n/a	n/a
START	a	nsd	n/a
SUBST	n/a	a	nsd
SYSLEVEL	a	n/a	n/a
SYSLOG	a	n/a	n/a
TIME	a	nsd	nsd
TREE	a	nsd	nsd
TYPE	a	nsd	nsd
UNDELETE	a	nsd	nsd
UNPACK	a	nsd	n/a
VER	a	nsd	nsd
VERIFY	a	nsd	nsd
VIEW	a	n/a	n/a
VMDISK	n/a	a	n/a
VOL	a	nsd	nsd
XCOPY	a	sd	sd

HOW THIS BOOK IS ORGANIZED

The first four sections in this book cover how to use the OS/2 graphical user interface. Part I describes how to install and configure OS/2 on your computer. Part II details the workplace shell and shows you how to use the windows, dialog boxes, and pull-down menus that make up OS/2's graphical user interface. Part III describes how to use the application programs included with OS/2, including the Database, the Spreadsheet, and the time-management applications. Part IV shows you how you can run your MS-DOS and Microsoft Windows programs under OS/2.

The last three sections of the book detail all the commands you can use from the command prompt, in your CONFIG.SYS file, and in your batch programming. Part V lists all the commands you can use at the OS/2 and OS/2 DOS-session command lines, with examples of command syntax and instructions on how to use the optional switches. Any major differences in usage between OS/2 DOS and MS-DOS are summarized for each command individually. Part VI lists all the commands you can use in your OS/2 CONFIG.SYS file to configure your computer system and computing environment. Part VII lists the batch-programming commands.

SYNTAX DESCRIPTIONS

Syntax descriptions are used throughout Parts V, VI, and VII to show just how to use a particular command. OS/2 commands are shown in **BOLD UPPERCASE** letters, and may be followed by any optional parameters, shown in their order of entry. Any required placeholders are shown in ***bold lowercase italic***, while optional parameters are shown in *standard lowercase italic*. Any optional switches are shown as */switches*, and are described in full in the text for that command.

ICONS

Icons are used to show that a command is available in an OS/2 session or an OS/2 DOS session, or both. You will see the following icons used throughout Parts V, VI, and VII of this book.

  Indicates that a command is available at the OS/2 command prompt.

DOS Indicates that a command is available at the DOS prompt.

If a command is available at both the OS/2 and the DOS command prompts, you will see both icons.

OS/2 VERSIONS COVERED BY THIS BOOK

This book covers OS/2 Version 2.0, released in the Spring of 1992, and OS/2 Version 2.1, released in 1993.

OS/2 2.0 was released in March of 1992, and introduced the object-oriented graphical user interface known as the desktop, or workplace shell. The desktop supported drag-and-drop operations and provided a suite of small but powerful productivity applications.

OS/2 2.1 was released as an upgrade in 1993, and contains many significant improvements and upgrades. For one, Version 2.1 supports Microsoft Windows 3.1 programs, including programs that require Windows Enhanced mode—programs that would not run under OS/2 2.0 now run without hesitation.

Support for hardware devices is also much better in 2.1, and the setup and installation of SCSI interface cards and CD-ROMs is much more straightforward than before.

Other features new in Version 2.1 include a desktop fax productivity application, support for 256-color SVGA boards, Personal Computer Memory Card International Association (PCMCIA) input/output devices, enhanced support for pen-based systems, the MultiMedia Presentation Manager (MMPM/2), support for the Advanced Power Management (APM) specification for battery-powered computers, and better support for OS/2 as an AS/400 client with a PCSupport program.

Part I

Installing and Configuring OS/2

This section first describes the OS/2 installation options and then goes on to cover how you can change and configure OS/2 system settings.

PREPARING TO INSTALL OS/2

Installing OS/2 is simple enough, though there are rather a lot of floppy disks in the box. The installation program guides you through the process step by step, asking you to insert the appropriate disks. A complete installation takes about an hour. Many computer vendors, including IBM and several of the mail-order companies, are installing OS/2 before they sell you the computer, and this is by far the easiest way to get your copy of OS/2. If you want to install it yourself, there are just a couple of decisions you should make before you start.

CHOOSING A FILE SYSTEM

When you install OS/2 you can choose to use a file system on your hard disk that is compatible with DOS 5 (and earlier versions of DOS) called *File Allocation Table* (FAT), or you can elect to use the OS/2 *High Performance File System* (HPFS). MS-DOS 5 cannot recognize files created by HPFS, but OS/2 can recognize MS-DOS 5 files as well as files created under FAT and by HPFS.

If you want to share files between OS/2 and a version of DOS that is independent of the OS/2 DOS sessions, choose the FAT option so that you will be able to swap files backwards and forwards or between different computers without any problems.

If you will only use OS/2 and OS/2 applications, and will never swap files with an MS-DOS system, choose the HPFS instead. HPFS is optimized for accessing large hard disks quickly, it supports file names of up to 254 characters in length, and it allows for additional extended file attributes. An extended attribute is a mechanism that allows an application to attach information to a file or directory. Extended attributes can be used to store notes about files, categorize the contents of a file, describe the format of data contained in a file, or append additional data to a file.

HPFS can only be used on hard disks; you cannot format a floppy disk with HPFS. To use HPFS you will have to format the hard disk or partition, and this process will destroy any information already on the disk. Make a backup of your hard disk before you start the installation process, then restore the files from the backup when the installation is complete.

USING THE BOOT MANAGER

If you want to install several operating systems on your computer and switch between them easily, consider using the OS/2 Boot Manager option. When you install the Boot Manager, every time you start your computer a menu will appear. This menu asks you to choose the operating system you want to use. You make your choice, and that operating system is started.

To install the Boot Manager, you must establish several partitions on your hard disk, and specify which operating system will run from which partition. When the OS/2 installation is complete, you can install the other operating systems. Again, if you decide to use the Boot Manager option, make a complete backup of all the files on your hard disk before you start the installation process, and reload them when the installation is complete.

HARDWARE REQUIREMENTS

To run OS/2 you must have at least an 80386 (or better) 32-bit processor in your computer. A partial installation of OS/2 occupies approximately 16MB of hard disk space, while a full installation takes about 30MB of free space. Remember that these space requirements are for just the operating system; if you add application programs, as you surely will, or if you want to install other operating systems, you will have to factor in the space that these programs will take.

You need at least 4MB of memory for OS/2, but add more memory if you can; 6MB or 8MB will give better performance. To use OS/2's graphical user interface, you also need a mouse or a trackball. You can install OS/2 from floppy disks or from a CD ROM.

INSTALLING OS/2
AS A SINGLE OPERATING SYSTEM

When you install OS/2 as the only operating system on your hard
disk, you can install it either on a new unused hard disk, or as an upgrade to an earlier version of OS/2. If you are making an upgrade
the installation program will update the appropriate OS/2 system
files, but will not affect your application programs or data files.
With OS/2 as the only operating system on your hard disk, you can
run OS/2 applications, Microsoft Windows applications, and
MS-DOS applications.

INSTALLING OS/2 ALONGSIDE MS-DOS

Another installation option is to add OS/2 to a system that already
has a version of MS-DOS installed on it. This gives you the option
of switching between MS-DOS and OS/2 should you need to; some
poorly written DOS programs do not run well under OS/2. With
this option, you can run OS/2 applications, DOS and Windows applications under OS/2 software emulation, as well as MS-DOS
applications.

The disadvantage of this flexibility is that you have to reboot the
computer when you change from OS/2 to MS-DOS. An OS/2 feature known as Dual Boot handles this for you and you can switch
from one operating system to the other from either the DOS or the
OS/2 command line by using the BOOT command (see Part V,
"OS/2 Commands," for more information on this command), or
from the OS/2 desktop by selecting the Dual Boot icon from the
Command Prompts folder.

To use Dual Boot you must make additions to your DOS AUTO-
EXEC.BAT and CONFIG.SYS files before you start to install OS/2.
Add the following lines to AUTOEXEC.BAT:

```
SET COMSPEC=C:\DOS\COMMAND.COM
PATH C:\DOS
APPEND=C:\DOS
COPY C:\DOS\COMMAND.COM C:\ >NUL
```

If you are using MS-DOS 4 or later, be sure to add these commands before the

C:\DOS\DOSSHELL

command.

Add this line to your CONFIG.SYS file:

SHELL=C:\DOS\COMMAND.COM /P

Finally, make sure that CONFIG.SYS and AUTOEXEC.BAT are the only files in your root directory. Then install any MS-DOS or Microsoft Windows application programs you want to add to your system, and you are ready to start the OS/2 installation program.

INSTALLING SEVERAL OPERATING SYSTEMS

The last installation option gives you the most flexibility. The Boot Manager lets you install several operating systems on your hard disk, and when you start your computer running, a menu asks you to choose the operating system you want to run. This kind of setup is particularly useful for programmers and application developers who have to use several different operating environments. Installing the Boot Manager is considered to be an advanced procedure because you may have to reformat and repartition your hard disk, depending on its original structure. See the *OS/2 Installation Guide* for more information.

RUNNING THE OS/2 INSTALLATION PROGRAM

To start the OS/2 installation program, place the floppy disk marked "Installation Diskette" in drive A and reboot the computer. You are prompted by screen messages to remove and replace floppy disks as needed during the installation process. As information is displayed on the screen, you can either accept it or change it; accepting and using the standard defaults will work in almost all circumstances. When the basic installation is complete, you will be asked to reboot the computer, and when you do you will see the OS/2 Installation and Setup window on the screen. This window contains the following choices:

- Learn how to use a mouse

- Install preselected features

- Install all features

- Select features and install

Use the ↓ key to highlight your selection, then press the Enter key. With the mouse, click on the selection you want, then click on the OK button. You can look at the mouse tutorial now, or you can wait until later because this tutorial is part of the larger OS/2 tutorial on the desktop. Choose the installation that meets your needs from the options offered in this window. If you do not install certain features now but later find that you need them, you can add them by using Selective Install from the System Setup folder. This procedure is described in the next section under the heading "Selective Install."

If you have MS-DOS or Microsoft Windows applications installed on your hard disk, you can migrate them to the OS/2 environment. This procedure is described in the next section under the heading "Migrate Applications."

When you have completed the OS/2 installation, restart your computer, and the OS/2 tutorial will be displayed on your screen. Click on the Next button or press the Enter key to start the tutorial. If you'd rather skip the tutorial, click on the Exit button to go directly to the OS/2 desktop.

CONFIGURING OS/2

If you want to change something in your OS/2 setup, or you have decided to add a feature that you originally chose not to install, open the OS/2 System icon, then choose System Setup from inside this folder, and you will see the icons shown in Figure I.1.

Figure I.1: System Setup—Icon View

To start one of these programs or objects, double-click on the appropriate icon, and a window opens containing choices you can make. When you are done, double-click on the small title-bar icon in the top left corner, and the window closes again. Your settings will remain in effect for subsequent OS/2 sessions.

COLOR PALETTE

Color Palette lets you choose the color used on the desktop. Select a color, then drag it to the object that you want to color and release the mouse button.

Select Edit Color to change the colors using a color wheel and either the red/green/blue or the hue/saturation/brightness color model. As you move the crosshairs on the color wheel, you change the properties of the color you selected. If you don't like the color you invented, use the Undo button to restore the color back to its original values.

COUNTRY

Country lets you change the way that the time, date, number and currency formats are shown in OS/2. Just click on one of the tabs down the right side of the window to open the appropriate item.

DEVICE DRIVER INSTALL

This selection guides you though adding a device driver to OS/2 from a device support disk provided by the manufacturer of a particular piece of hardware. For more information, see the DDINSTAL command in Part V, "OS/2 Commands."

FONT PALETTE

The Font Palette displays examples of some of the fonts available on your system. You can drag a font sample from this window, drop it onto any text on the desktop, and that text will change into the font in the chosen font sample. Hold down the Alt key as you drag if you want to make a system-wide change. Select Edit Font to add, delete, or edit font samples.

KEYBOARD

Use Keyboard to change the following settings:

- Keyboard repeat rate
- Keyboard repeat delay rate
- Cursor blink rate
- Keys used to display pop-up menus and editing title text
- Special settings

MIGRATE APPLICATIONS

Use this special option to search your hard disk for MS-DOS, Windows, or OS/2 programs that you want to see represented as a folder on the desktop. A program can migrate to the desktop if an entry for it appears in a file called DATABASE.DAT.

MOUSE

Use Mouse to change the following settings:

- Double-click speed
- Tracking speed
- Right- or left-handed mouse

SCHEME PALETTE

Use Scheme Palette to change colors and fonts for all the parts of a window, including window text, menu bars, screen backgrounds, even the width of the horizontal or vertical window borders. To make a color change system-wide, hold down the Alt key as you drag a color to an object.

SELECTIVE INSTALL

When you open Selective Install, a window opens offering the same choices you saw during the installation of OS/2:

- Mouse
- Serial Device Support
- Primary Display
- Secondary Display
- Country
- Keyboard
- CD-ROM Device Support
- SCSI Adapter Support
- Printer

If you click on the Mouse check box, you can choose one option from the following list:

- PS/2 (™) Style Pointing Device
- Bus Style Mouse

- InPort Style Mouse
- Serial Pointing Device
- Logitech (™) Serial Mouse
- Other Pointing Device for Mouse Port
- No pointing device support

Make a selection, then click on OK to select the serial port that your mouse is attached to.

If you choose Keyboard, you can select a keyboard layout from 28 different options. If you select Country, you can select a code page, or character set, from 31 different options. If you choose Primary Display, you can choose from the following:

- Color Graphics Adapter
- Enhanced Graphics Adapter
- PS/2 Display Adapter
- Video Graphics Array
- Display Adapter 8514/A
- Extended Graphics Array
- Super Video Graphics Array (SVGA)
- Other

If you choose Secondary Display, you have two more choices: Monochrome/Printer Adapter and None.

Select OK when you are done with this list to open the next window, shown in Figure I.2.

Choose the appropriate CD-ROM, Small Computer System Interface (SCSI) adapter, and printer from the choices available under these headings. To select an option, click on the appropriate check box; to deselect an option, click on the check box a second time.

Each option shows the amount of disk space it will occupy if you choose to make the installation, and the selections at the top of the list have More buttons, indicating that further settings or choices are available.

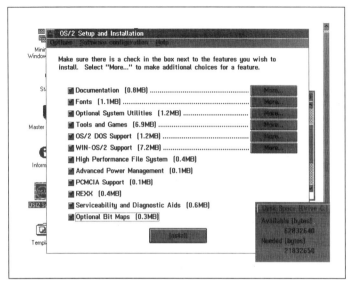

Figure I.2: OS/2 Setup and installation optional features

The Options menu contains selections you can use to start the installation process, format a disk, or go directly to the OS/2 command prompt. The Software configuration menu contains two advanced items for experienced users who want to fine-tune OS/2 or DOS system parameters.

When you have completed your selections, use Install from the Options menu, or click on the Install button. You are asked to insert the appropriate floppy disks as the installation process proceeds.

SOUND

Use Sound to turn the warning beep off.

SPOOLER

Spooler lets you specify a new path for storing spool files waiting to be printed. Any changes you make become effective immediately.

SYSTEM

Use System to change the OS/2 settings for any of the following:

- Confirmation messages on file or folder deletions, file renaming, and other related items

- Title clashes where an item is added to a folder that already contains an object of the same name

- Window settings for animation, window behavior, and so on

- Enable or disable Print Screen

- Logo display times

- System name and icon

SYSTEM CLOCK

Use the Clock settings to:

- Set the date or time

- Set an alarm

- Control the clock window

- Choose between an analog and digital clock display

WIN-OS/2 SETUP

New in OS/2 2.1, WIN-OS/2 lets you change the WIN-OS/2 settings and session types for all WIN-OS/2 sessions. You can also select a public or private clipboard or dynamic data exchange between OS/2, DOS, and WIN-OS/2 sessions.

Part II

The Workplace Shell

This section describes the elements of the OS/2 object-oriented graphical user interface known as the *workplace shell* and shows you how to use part of the workplace shell, the *desktop*, to perform common everyday tasks.

THE OS/2 USER INTERFACE

OS/2 is not just an operating system. It also contains a complete, object-oriented graphical user interface known as the workplace shell. The workplace shell ensures consistency between applications, which is what makes it so valuable. Once you can perform a task in one application, you can perform that same task everywhere else without having to learn a new technique. The workplace shell is a collection of different objects that all work in a similar way.

THE ELEMENTS OF THE WORKPLACE SHELL

When you work with the workplace shell, you are working with four main kinds of objects:

- Program objects, representing applications such as word processors, spreadsheets, and so on.

- Folder objects, representing collections of other objects. A folder may represent a directory and contain a collection of files, or it may represent a group of programs. Folders can also contain other folders. The OS/2 desktop is a special kind of folder, because it is always open.

- Data-file objects, including information such as text, memos, letters, spreadsheets, video and sound.

- Device objects, such as printers, plotters, modems, and facsimile machines.

Many of the objects seen on the desktop are represented by icons, or small pictures. Some of these icons resemble the device they represent, such as the Drive A icon; others represent folders and application programs and may look rather more exotic.

USING THE OS/2 DESKTOP

A special folder, known as the desktop, fills the entire screen, and contains other objects, including folders and device objects. The following objects and folders are usually found on the desktop:

- OS/2 System folder. This folder contains other folders, including the Startup folder, Productivity folder, Games folder, Command Prompts folder, System Setup folder, and the Drives folder.

- Information folder. This folder contains the README text file, REXX Information, the OS/2 Command Reference and Tutorial, and the Glossary. The first time OS/2 starts after the installation is complete, the tutorial opens on the desktop. You can view it then, or at any other convenient time.

- Start Here object. This object contains a set of topics and related help information.

- Master Help Index object. This contains the main OS/2 help information.

- Templates folder. This folder contains examples of different kinds of objects you can use to help you create a new object of that type on the desktop. Just drag a copy of the object to another place on the desktop.

- Drive A object. This object displays the contents of the floppy disk in drive A.

- Shredder object. When you drop an object onto the Shredder, it asks you to confirm that you want to delete the object. If you answer yes, the Shredder immediately deletes the object.

- Printer object. You can drag objects to the printer icon and print their contents.

Your desktop may also show folders containing OS/2, DOS, and Windows programs.

Figure II.1 shows a typical arrangement with the OS/2 System folder open on the desktop.

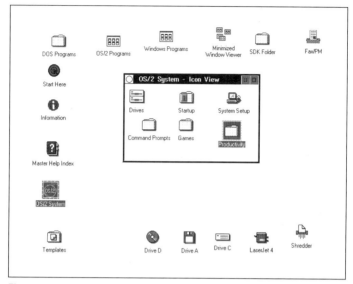

Figure II.1: The OS/2 System folder open on the desktop

The OS/2 graphical user interface is designed for use with a mouse, or similar pointing device such as a track ball. There are several ways you can use the mouse:

• Clicking the left mouse button (button 1) selects an object or an item from a menu.

• Clicking the right mouse button (button 2) on an object opens the object's pop-up menu.

• Double-clicking the left mouse button (pressing the mouse button twice in quick succession when the mouse pointer is over an object) opens the object.

• Dragging is a way to move an object. Place the mouse pointer on the object, then press and hold down the right mouse button. Now move the mouse to the object's new location while continuing to hold down the button, and release the mouse button.

The OS/2 help information refers to the mouse buttons as button 1 and button 2, rather than just left and right. This is because you can configure the mouse to work any way you want, left- or right-handed. Throughout the rest of this book, I refer to the left and right mouse buttons in their original configuration.

You can also use the mouse in combination with the Ctrl key on the keyboard; see the heading "Copying and Moving Files and Folders" later in this section for more information.

When you click the right mouse button on an object, you open that object's pop-up menu. This menu contains the operations you can perform with that object. The basic selections in this menu include the following: Open, Help, Create Another, Copy, Move, Create Shadow, and Find. Depending on the type of object you are working with, you may see other selections in the pop-up menu, including Select, Sort, Arrange, Window, Close, or Delete. You can even add your own entries into this menu; see the heading "Using the Settings Notebooks" later in this section for more information.

To open the pop-up menu for the desktop, just click the right mouse button on a blank part of the desktop not occupied by an object or a window. There are two special entries in the desktop pop-up menu: Lockup Now and Shut Down. See the headings "Securing Your Desktop" and "Shutting Down Your Computer" later in this section for more information.

Some menu selections show an arrow symbol pointing to the right. When you click on this arrow, you open a secondary, or *cascading menu*. If the arrow looks like a button, one of the selections in the cascading menu has a check mark next to it that indicates the default action taken when you click on your original choice. If the arrow is not a button but is flat, you have to make a choice from the items in the cascaded menu.

USING WINDOWS

When you work with the desktop, objects are often displayed in a window. These windows may display other objects, folders, files or directories, but the individual elements found in all windows are essentially the same. As an example, Figure II.2 shows the System Setup folder with the following elements:

- Window border. When two or more windows are open, the border of the active window is shown highlighted in a different color. You can drag the border to resize the window.

- Title bar. The bar across the top of the window contains the window title, the title-bar icon, and the minimize and maximize buttons. You can drag the title bar if you want to move the entire window rather than just resize it.

- Title-bar icon. The title-bar icon at the left end of the title bar shows a reduced icon for the object displayed in the window. Click on this icon to open the pop-up menu, or double-click on it to close the window.

- Minimize button. Click on this button to minimize the window; the minimized window is moved into the Minimized Window Viewer object to avoid cluttering up your desktop.

- Maximize button. Click on this button to expand the window to the largest possible size, usually the whole screen.

- Scroll bar. When all the information in a window cannot be shown at the same time because the window is too small, scroll bars appear across the bottom and down the right side of the window. Click on the arrowheads on the scroll bar to move through the information one line at a time, or hold down the mouse button to scroll through the information until you find what you are looking for.

- Slider box. You can use the slider box to move one page at a time through the information in a window. Click above, below, to the right, or to the left of the slider bar to move to the next page.

Application programs may add many more elements to a window, including a menu bar containing pull-down menus, a tool bar for access to graphical controls, dialog boxes for parameter selection, and command or push buttons for additional options.

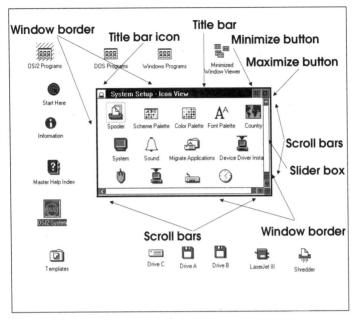

Figure II.2: The parts of a window

SELECTING OBJECTS

To select an object, move the mouse cursor onto the object and click the left mouse button. This highlights the object to confirm that you have selected it. To select several objects, move the mouse pointer onto the object and click the left mouse button as before, but this time do not release the mouse button, but move the mouse pointer over the other objects you want to select. You will see each of them highlighted in turn as they are selected. Release the mouse button when you have completed your selections.

To select noncontiguous objects, hold down the Ctrl key and click with the left mouse button on the objects you want.

Use these methods to select one or more items in a folder when you want to perform the same operation on a group of objects.

USING THE WINDOW LIST

The Window List shows the names of all the objects you are using and all the programs you are running. Hidden and minimized windows are also shown in the Window List. To switch from one object to another using the Window List:

1. Move the mouse cursor to an empty area of the desktop.

2. Click *both* mouse buttons together; this is sometimes described as *chording*.

3. Double-click on the object you want to make current, or the minimized window you want to maximize.

4. Press the Escape key or double-click on the title-bar icon to dismiss the Window List from the desktop.

The titles of hidden windows are also shown in the Window List; see the heading "Hiding Windows" later in this section for more information.

ONLINE HELP

There are many ways you can access OS/2's abundant online help information. Many of the pop-up menus and dialog boxes have a help entry containing immediate information. You can also access specific help information on a pop-up menu selection by pressing (but not releasing) the left mouse button, then pressing the F1 function key. If you want more information, you can go to the Master Help Index.

The Master Help Index contains thousands of topics arranged into alphabetical order. These topics are displayed in a form like that of a notepad with tabs down the right side. Click on a letter to go directly to the group of entries that begin with that letter. Information for that entry is shown in a window that opens to the right of the Master Help Index, as shown in Figure II.3.

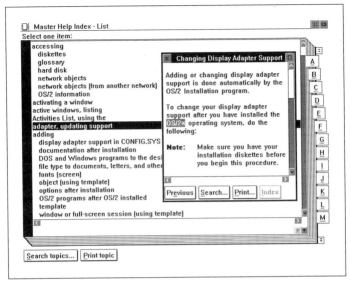

Figure II.3: The Master Help Index

At the end of the help text, you will see several topic headings listed under Related Information. Double-click on one of these items to open the associated help entry.

To search the Master Help Index for an entry, click on the Search Topics button. Enter the text you want to search for into the Search String box, then click on the Search button. When matches are found, they are listed in the Matched Items box; double-click on one of these matches to display its help information. When you have located the right topic, you can print the entry by clicking on the Print Topic button.

The Information folder on the desktop contains the OS/2 Tutorial, the Glossary, the OS/2 Command Reference, REXX Information, and the README file.

KEYBOARD SHORTCUTS

You can also use the keyboard with the workplace shell; there are keyboard equivalents for all the mouse-based operations. To help in this, each menu selection has one letter underlined. Just type that letter from the keyboard to select the option from the menu. Because several menu selections may start with the same letter, the choice of letters for some of the keyboard shortcuts may be less than intuitive. Table II.1 lists all the OS/2 system functions you can perform from the keyboard. Table II.2 lists the keys you can use when you are working with objects. Table II.3 shows the keys you can use when you are working with windows. Table II.4 lists the keys you can use within a desktop help window. Finally, Table II.5 shows the keys you can use when you are working with the Master Help Index. A plus sign, as in Ctrl+Alt+Del, means that you must hold down the specified keys together.

USING THE SETTINGS NOTEBOOKS

Every object has an associated settings notebook, opened from the object's pop-up menu. These notebooks let you look at and change the settings that control how the object behaves. They are called notebooks because that's what they look like on the screen. Figure II.4 shows the Drive C Settings notebook as an example. Tabs on the right side of the notebook divide the different settings into functional groups, and each of these groups may contain several pages of information. The number and the names of these tabs depend on the type of object you are working with.

Table II.1: Shortcut Keys for System Tasks

Key	Function
Ctrl+Alt+Del	Restarts the operating system
Alt+Tab	Switches to the next window
Alt+Esc	Switches to the next window or full-screen session
Ctrl+Esc	Opens the Window List
F1	Opens help

Table II.2: Shortcut Keys Used with Objects

Key	Function
Arrow keys	Moves between objects
Spacebar	Selects an object
Enter	Opens an object or accepts a menu selection
Esc	Closes a pop-up menu, or cancels a mouse selection
Shift+F10	Opens the selected object's pop-up menu
Home	Selects the first option in a pop-up menu
End	Selects the last option in a pop-up menu
Underlined letter	Selects a specific choice from a menu

Table II.3: Shortcut Keys Used with Windows

Key	Function
Alt+Spacebar	Opens the pop-up menu for a window
Alt+F4	Closes a window
Alt+F7	Lets you move a window using the arrow keys
Alt+F8	Lets you size a window using the arrow keys
Alt+F9	Minimizes a window
Alt+F10	Maximizes a window
Alt+F11	Hides a window
PgUp, PgDn	Moves through the contents of a window one page at a time

Table II.4: Shortcut Keys for a Desktop Help Window

Key	Function
F2	Displays general help information
F9	Displays information for help keys, system keys, windows keys, object keys, and selection keys
F11	Displays Help index
Shift+F10	Displays the help topic "Help for Using the Help Facility"
Tab	Moves to the next highlighted help topic. Press the Enter key to display the associated help information
Esc	Displays the previous help information

Table II.5: Shortcut Keys Used with the Master Help Index

Key	Function
Enter	Opens the Master Help Index
Arrow keys	Moves through the help topics, one at a time
PgUp, PgDn	Moves through the help topics one page at a time
Any letter	Moves to the first topic beginning with that letter
Alt+F6	Switches between an entry and the Master Help Index
Tab	Moves to the next highlighted help topic. Press the Enter key to display the associated help information
Esc	Closes the help window

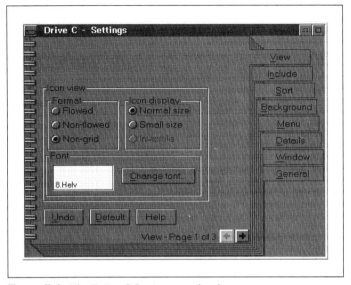

Figure II.4: The Drive C Settings notebook

You open the settings notebook for the desktop by right-clicking anywhere that is not in use on the desktop. This opens the desktop pop-up menu. Then click on the arrow next to Open and choose the Settings option. To open the Settings notebook for any other object, right-click on the object, then choose Open, followed by Settings.

Each settings notebook contains tabs specific to the object you are working with; similar objects usually have similar settings. For example, program objects have the following tabs, or groups, of settings:

- Program contains the path, file name, and directory name for the object.

- Session defines the type of session the program can run in: OS/2 full screen, OS/2 Window, DOS full screen, DOS Window, WIN-OS/2 full screen, or WIN-OS/2 window. A WIN-OS/2 program can also run in a separate WIN-OS/2 session.

- Association defines the types or names of data-file objects linked to the program. See the heading "Associating Objects" later in this section for more on how to establish associations.

- Window controls the behavior of minimized windows.

- General contains the program title and icon information.

A disk drive object may contain all of these tabs and add several more, including the following:

- View controls the icon display and font type used.

- Include specifies the kinds of objects included in a view.

- Sort specifies a sort order of the objects contained in a view.

- Background specifies an image to display in the background of any folder, including the desktop folder.

- Menu controls the user-defined additions to an object's pop-up menu. Select the Primary pop-up menu from the Available menus field, then use the Create Another button if you want to add an item to the Primary pop-up menu.

- Details displays the current information for the selected hard or floppy disk.

If a tab contains more than one page, you will see a page count just above the left- and right-facing arrow buttons at the bottom right of the page. Use the arrow buttons to move from one page to another, or from one tab to the next.

When you make a change in a settings notebook, that change takes effect immediately; you do not have to save the change. If you decide to remove a change, click on the Undo button. To return to the original value for that item, click on the Default button.

USING THE DESKTOP

The following sections describe how you can use the desktop to perform everyday file-, disk-, and program-management tasks.

STARTING AND CLOSING APPLICATIONS

To start an OS/2 application, just double-click on the appropriate object and the program will start running in its own window. If you want the application to use the whole screen, click on the maximize button in the top right corner of the original window. You can also select the object you want, then use the Open selection from the pop-up menu to start the program running.

Another way to start an application is to double-click on a data object; this opens the data object (letter, memo, data file) and simultaneously starts the program associated with that data object. See the heading "Associating Objects" later in this section for more information.

You can also start an application by typing its file name at the OS/2 command prompt.

To close an application, click on the title-bar icon to open the menu, then choose the Close selection. You can also type Alt+F4 or double-click on the title-bar icon to close the application.

For more information on working with Microsoft Windows and MS-DOS application programs, see Part IV, "Running OS/2, DOS, and Windows Programs under OS/2."

HIDING WINDOWS

Some windows have a *hide button* at the end of the title bar, to the left of the maximize button, that is shaped like a plus sign (+). Click on this button to hide the window. Other applications may have a hide entry in title-bar icon menu that you can access by pressing Alt+F11. In either case, the name of the window is added to the

28   The Workplace Shell

Window List so that you can still access the window, even though it is hidden.

TILING AND CASCADING WINDOWS

You can arrange open windows by hand if you wish, by dragging them into place with the mouse, but it is easier and faster to use the Tile or Cascade commands.

When you tile windows, they are arranged side by side on the desktop with the active window placed at the top left corner of the desktop. Figure II.5 shows several tiled windows on the desktop.

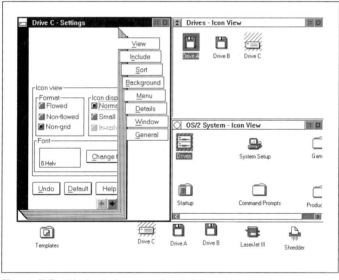

Figure II.5: Tiled windows on the desktop

To tile windows, follow these steps:

1. Open the Window List.

2. Select the windows you want to tile.

3. Place the mouse pointer over one of the window titles in the Window List, and click the right mouse button to open the pop-up menu for this window.

4. Select Tile from the pop-up menu.

When you cascade windows, they appear arranged one behind the next, with only their title bars showing. The active window is always displayed at the front of the stack. To cascade a set of windows, follow the steps given above for tiling windows, but choose the Cascade option instead of the Tile option. Figure II.6 shows several cascaded windows on the desktop.

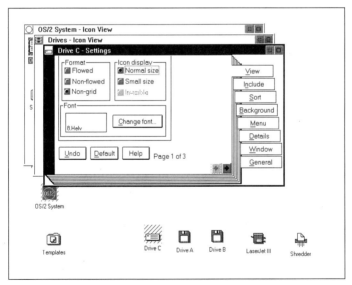

Figure II.6: Cascaded windows on the desktop

If you want to tile or cascade all windows open on the desktop, use the Select All option from the Window List title-bar icon menu, rather than selecting each window separately.

ARRANGING ICONS

You can also arrange the icons on the desktop or in an open folder by hand, dragging them one by one then dropping them at the new location, or you can make the system place the icons in a default arrangement for you.

To arrange all the icons on the desktop:

1. Open the desktop pop-up menu by clicking the right mouse button on an empty area of the desktop.

2. Select the Arrange option from the pop-up menu.

To arrange the icons in an open window:

1. Move the mouse pointer into the window and right-click the mouse.

2. Select the Arrange option from the menu.

You can also use the Sort menu option to arrange the icons by name, date, time, and so on.

SHUTTING DOWN YOUR COMPUTER

Before you turn your computer off, you *must* make sure that OS/2 is closed in a logical way, and you do that with the Shut Down command. If you do not use Shut Down every time you turn off your computer, you will lose data, and the operating system may not be able to start properly when you turn your computer back on again.

Shut Down makes sure that any information currently in the hard disk cache buffer is saved on the hard disk, and that all open windows are closed. Shut Down also checks all sessions for unsaved data before starting the actual shut down process. All of this status information is saved, so that next time you start OS/2, all objects that were open can reopen and appear in the same view. Many OS/2 application programs can also save their own state, and therefore can resume exactly where they left off.

To shut down your computer before you turn it off:

1. Click the right mouse button on any blank part of the desktop to open the desktop pop-up menu.

2. Select Shut Down.

3. Respond to any messages displayed on the screen as shut down proceeds, closing any open applications.

4. When you see the final message telling you it is now safe to turn off your computer, turn it off or press Ctrl+Alt+Del to restart it once again.

SECURING YOUR DESKTOP

You can use the Lockup Now command from the desktop pop-up menu to make your computer screen go blank and lock the keyboard. You can also use this command to establish a desktop password if you wish. To use Lockup Now:

1. Open the desktop pop-up menu by clicking the right mouse button on an empty part of the desktop.

2. Click on the arrow button next to the Open selection, then choose Settings from the cascaded menu.

3. Click on the Lockup tab on the right side of the Desktop Settings notebook. This notebook has three pages.

4. On the first page, enable or disable the automatic lockup, then specify a timeout period in minutes. This timeout represents the length of time that OS/2 will wait after your last interaction before automatically locking the system.

5. On the next page of the notebook, specify the picture or *bit map* you want to display on the screen after the timeout expires. The file called OS2LOGO.BMP contains the OS/2 logo.

6. On page three of the notebook, enter the password you want to use to unlock the desktop. If you forget this password, you will have to restart your computer, then enter a new password before the timeout expires.

7. Double-click on the title-bar icon to close the Desktop Settings notebook.

When the timeout expires, or when you use Lockup Now from the
desktop pop-up menu, the bit map you chose is shown on
the screen, along with a small padlock icon and a Help button.
Click on the Help button to open a small help box on the screen
containing instructions on how to enter your password. If you wait
long enough, eventually the bit map will disappear from the screen
to avoid burning in the image on the screen, and all you will see
will be the padlock icon moving about the screen. Press any key on
the keyboard to redisplay the bit map and the Help button.

ASSOCIATING OBJECTS

You can create a special kind of link, known as an *association*, between a program and one or more data files. This association lets
you open both the program and the data file simply by selecting the
data file. For example, you can associate a letter file with your word
processing program, or you can associate all your text documents
with the word processor; the choice is yours. By default, all data
files are initially associated with the OS/2 System Editor, but you
can easily change that. Here are the steps:

1. Open the pop-up menu for the program you want to work
    with by clicking on the program icon.

2. Click on the arrow next to the Open selection, then choose
    Settings from the cascaded menu.

3. When the Settings notebook opens, click on the Associa-
    tion tab.

4. Type in the file name of the data-file object you want to as-
    sociate with this program, then click on the Add button.
    Alternatively, to associate all data-file objects that share a
    common file-name extension, enter that extension and
    click on Add. For example, enter ***.DOC** to associate all
    data-file objects whose names end in .DOC. Finally, you
    can choose one or more of the object types from the Avail-
    able Types list, and then select the Add button.

CREATING WORK-AREA FOLDERS

A slightly different kind of association, one that allows you to group objects related to a specific task, is known as a *work-area folder*. For example, you can create a work-area folder to hold everything associated with a particular project, including data-file objects containing early versions of your report, the actual report itself, the word processing program you used, and a specially configured printer.

Work-area folders have several features that makes working with them very easy:

- When you close the folder, all the windows that belong to the objects contained within the folder are also closed automatically.

- When you next open the folder, all the windows are reopened just as they were when you closed the folder.

- If you hide the work-area folder window, all other windows belonging to objects within the work-area folder are also hidden automatically.

- If you minimize a work-area folder, only the icon for the folder is displayed; the windows that belong to the objects inside the folder are not displayed.

- A work-area folder is considered to be a single object in the Window List, so that you can manage all the objects in the folder with a single action.

You can create a work-area folder by converting an existing folder or by using a template. Either way, follow these steps:

1. Open the pop-up menu for the folder.

2. Select the arrow to the right of the Open selection, then choose Settings.

3. Click on the File tab in the folder settings notebook.

4. Click on the Work Area check box on page one.

5. Double-click on the title-bar icon to close the notebook.

CHANGING THE VIEW

You can look at the information contained in a folder in three different ways by using Icon view, Tree view, or Details view.

- Icon view shows the objects in the folder as different icons. Programs have their own special icons; files are assigned generic icons depending on the file type; text files, program files, and so on all have different icons; and directories are shown as folders. Icon view makes it very easy to move or rearrange the objects inside a folder.

- Tree view shows the objects in the folder arranged in a hierarchical fashion. It is most useful for displaying the contents of directories because it gives a good indication of how things are organized. Tree view is described in more detail in the next section, "Listing Files and Folders."

- Details view gives you all the information about each of the objects in the folder, including a tiny replica icon, the icon title, the real name (usually the file name), size, the last write time, the last access date and time, the create date and time, and the file attributes or flags.

To change the view, open the pop-up menu, select the arrow next to Open, then choose either Icon View, Tree View, or Details View.

LISTING FILES AND FOLDERS

To look at the files structure on a disk, open the Drives folder in the OS/2 System folder. You will find icons for each of the drives on your system inside the Drives folder. Drive A is always available directly from the desktop, and you can move other drives to the desktop too, if you wish.

By default, files and folders (or directories) are displayed in the Tree view to show off their hierarchical structure. At the top of the drive window, you will see a short summary of the free and total space available on the drive. The rest of the window is occupied by the display of folders and files inside those folders. A plus sign to the left of a folder indicates that there are other objects inside this folder; click on the icon to display the contents. A minus sign means that all the objects in the folder are displayed; click on this icon to collapse the structure. As you expand and contract this display, remember that nothing is happening to the actual files themselves; only the display is changing.

FINDING FILES AND FOLDERS

If you cannot see the file or folder you are looking for, you can use Find to help locate it. Open the pop-up menu for the folder, then click on Find to open the Find notebook, and enter the information needed to find your folder as follows:

1. Type the name of the folder that contains the folder you are searching for the Folder text field.

2. Click on the Locate button to open the Locate Folder notebook so you can specify where to start the search.

3. Back on the Find page, enter the name of the file or folder you are looking for into the Name field.

4. Specify the type of object you are looking for in the Type field.

5. Use the radio buttons at the bottom of this page to search just this folder or to search all subfolders.

6. Click on the Find button to start the search.

If you just search the current folder, Find automatically creates a Find Results folder on the desktop; if you search all subfolders, Find Results opens the folders that contain the objects you were looking for.

CREATING FILES AND FOLDERS

There are two ways you can create a new file or folder:

• Right-click on a folder to open the pop-up menu, then select the Create Another option. This creates a new folder with the same settings as the original.

• Open the Templates folder and drag the example folder to a new location. This creates an empty folder that you can customize as you wish.

Both of these operations work in the same way for creating new
data-file objects; in the Templates folder, choose the example data-
file object rather than the example folder.

COPYING AND MOVING FILES AND FOLDERS

When you copy an object, you create an exact replica of the original
object in a new location; when you move an object, you transfer it
from the original location to a new location. Copying or moving is
easiest with the mouse. Here are the steps for files or folders:

1. Open an icon view on the disk that contains the data-file
   objects or folders you want to move or copy.

2. Select the appropriate objects with the left mouse button.

3. To move the data file or folder, press and hold down the
   right mouse button while you drag the object to the target
   object. If you want to copy the object (and keep the
   original), hold down the Ctrl key on the keyboard as you
   drag the object to the new location.

4. Release the right mouse button, and the data-file object
   will be copied or moved to the new location.

You can also move or copy an object using selections from the pop-
up menu, as follows:

1. Right-click on the folder or file to open its pop-up menu.

2. Click on the Move or the Copy selection, depending on
   the type of operation you want to perform.

3. Select a tab on the notebook that corresponds to the destination object for this move or copy operation. Choose
   from:

   • An open folder
   • A related folder
   • The OS/2 desktop
   • A drive
   • A destination folder defined by a path statement

4. When you have specified a destination, click on either the Move button or the Copy button to complete the operation.

CREATING A SHADOW OF AN OBJECT

Sometimes it is useful to have two copies of the same object available on the desktop at the same time. The OS/2 mechanism that makes this possible is called a shadow. The data in a shadow is always the same as the data contained in the original, and any operation you perform on a shadow also occurs in the original. If you delete an object, you automatically delete its shadow. You can think of a shadow as being an alias for the original object.

To create a shadow copy of an object and its contents, follow these steps:

1. Select the object you want to shadow.

2. Press and hold down the Ctrl and Shift keys.

3. Press and hold down the right mouse button.

4. Drag the shadow of the object into any folder.

5. Release the right mouse button.

Alternatively, you can use the Create Shadow selection from the object's pop-up menu.

DELETING FILES AND FOLDERS

When you want to delete an object, you can drag it to the Shredder on the desktop or you can use the Delete selection in the pop-up menu. If you delete a folder, you also delete all of the folder's contents, including files and other folders.

To use the Shredder, select the object using the left mouse button, then drag the object and drop it onto the Shredder. A confirmation window opens to check that you really do want to delete this object; click on the Delete button and the object is history. Remember, however, that the Shredder is not a folder; you cannot recover objects from the Shredder.

Deleting with the pop-up menu takes just a few more steps:

1. Right-click on the object you want to delete to open its pop-up menu.

2. Choose the Delete selection.

3. Confirm your determination to delete this object with the Delete button.

4. If the object you are deleting is a folder, you will see an additional message asking if you are sure you want to delete the folder *and all of its contents*.

5. Click on Yes to proceed.

RENAMING OBJECTS

If you want to change an object's name, there are two methods you can use. If the object is a newly created copy, you can use this fast method of name editing:

1. Press and hold down the Alt key on the keyboard.

2. Click on the object whose name you want to change.

3. Release the Alt key, and use the Backspace and Delete keys on the keyboard to remove the old name. Then enter the new name.

4. Click on the object a second time to complete the renaming process.

Alternatively, you can select the object, then right-click on it to open its pop-up menu. Click on the arrow next to Open and then choose Settings to open the settings notebook. Click on the General tab and enter a new name or edit the existing name in the Title box at the top of the page. Double-click on the title-bar icon to close the settings notebook, and you will see that the object's name has changed.

COPYING FLOPPY DISKS

If you want to make an exact copy of a disk, you can use the Copy Disk command from a drive's pop-up menu. This command requires that both of the disks and the disk drives used in this operation be identical, both in terms of disk type and in capacity. If they are not identical, OS/2 aborts the copy and displays an error message.

If you want to copy the disk in drive A onto the disk in drive B, use the Copy Disk command in drive A's pop-up menu; use drive B's pop-up menu if you want to go the other way.

When you start this command, an OS/2 window opens on the screen to guide you through the duplication operation; when you are finished, you return to the desktop.

See the DISKCOPY command in Part V, "OS/2 Commands," for information on how to duplicate a floppy disk from the OS/2 or DOS command prompt.

FORMATTING A FLOPPY DISK

To format a new floppy disk, follow these steps:

1. Open the OS/2 System folder on the desktop.

2. Open the Drives folder and select the disk drive containing the disk you want to format.

3. Right-click on the drive icon to open its pop-up menu.

4. Click on Format Disk.

5. Enter the text you want to use as a disk label, select the appropriate capacity for the disk. If you are formatting a hard disk, choose between the FAT or the HPFS.

6. Click on the Format button to start the formatting process. A graphic shows the progress made by the format, and lists the total and free space on the disk when the format is complete.

Because the Drive A icon is always available on the desktop, you can cut out several of the steps listed above if you want to format a disk in this drive; just right-click on the drive icon to open its pop-up menu and choose Format Disk.

See the FORMAT command in Part V, "OS/2 Commands," for information on how to format a floppy disk from the OS/2 or DOS command prompt.

CHECKING A DISK

If you are about to install a large application and you want to be sure that there is enough free disk space before you start the installation process, it is useful to be able to check a disk for problems and to determine the amount of disk space still free for use. Here are the steps to follow:

1. Open the OS/2 System folder on the desktop.

2. Open the Drives folder and select the disk drive that contains the disk you want to check. If you want to check a floppy disk, insert it into the drive before you select the drive.

3. Right-click on the drive icon to open its pop-up menu.

4. Click on Check Disk, then click on the Check button. Click on the Write Corrections to Disk check box if you want to correct any disk problems this process finds.

The Check Disk-Results report displays the following information:

*   Type of file system in use on the disk

*   Total amount of disk space, in bytes

*   Free space remaining on the disk, in bytes

*   A pie chart showing the amount of space on the disk reserved for system files and the amount of space occupied by folders, user files, unusable areas on the disk, and extended attributes

Click on the Cancel button to dismiss this report.

See the CHKDSK command in Part V, "OS/2 Commands," for information on how to check a disk from the OS/2 or DOS command prompt.

PRINTING FROM THE DESKTOP

There are several methods you can use to print a file. If you have a printer (or plotter) installed on your system, you will see a printer icon on the desktop. If you use a network printer, you may find this icon in the Network folder rather than on the desktop.

The simplest way of printing a file is to drag it to the printer icon, but there are several other methods you can use:

- Selecting the Print option from the object's pop-up menu

- Using the Print command from an application program's File menu

- Using the PRINT or COPY commands from the OS/2 prompt

- Selecting the Print Topic button in a help window

- Pressing the Print Screen key on the keyboard

Each of these methods creates a *print job*, and if you open the printer object, you will see a window displaying the status of all the jobs waiting to be printed on your system. To delete one or more of these pending print jobs, open the pop-up menu for the job, and choose the Delete option. Select the Delete All Jobs option if you want to delete all of the pending print jobs. You can create one or more copies of a print job if you use the Copy command from the object's pop-up menu. Finally, if you want to print to a file rather than to the usual printer, open the object's pop-up menu, click on the arrow to the right of Open, and choose Settings. Select the Output tab, then choose Output to File. Double-click on the title-bar icon to close the settings notebook.

Part III

Using the OS/2 Productivity Applications

This section briefly describes each of the productivity and games programs supplied with OS/2 2.1. To locate these applications, open the OS/2 System folder on the desktop, then double-click on the Productivity folder or the Games folder. The icons contained in the Productivity folder are shown in Figure III.1; just double-click on an icon to open the application you want to use.

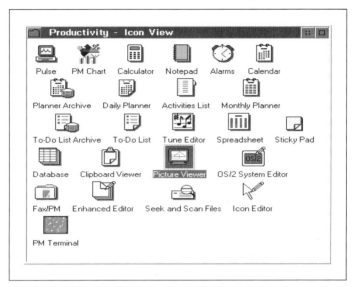

Figure III.1: Application icons in the Productivity folder

In the descriptions that follow, the applications are arranged in alphabetical order.

ACTIVITIES LIST

The Activities List lets you look at, but not change, all your Daily Planner entries. The only information you can't see is the empty time slots. You can copy or find entries, and you can sort activities by Planner Date or by Description.

See also Daily Planner.

ALARMS

The Alarms application lets you set or cancel a built-in alarm system. You can set an alarm for a specific day, hour, and minute, and then select a graphic element for display in a pop-up window and a tune fragment that will be played when the alarm goes off.

Use the Customize menu to specify the number of times the tune will be played and the length of time you want to use as the *snooze* period. You can also tie the alarms into a master planner file, so that the alarms in this file can be activated too.

When you schedule an activity using the Daily Planner, you can enter an alarm time from 0 to 59 minutes. This is the number of minutes before the activity start time you want the alarm to sound.

See also Daily Planner.

CALCULATOR

The Calculator mimics a hand-held calculator on the screen. You can enter numbers directly from the keyboard or by clicking on the calculator keys on the screen. The results of your calculations are shown on the paper tape or *tally roll*. If you use the memory register, its contents are displayed above the tally roll in a separate memory display. The Tally menu contains options for clearing and printing the tally roll, while the Customize menu contains options for configuring the calculator.

CALENDAR

The Calendar presents a concise view of your month. If you open a file created by the Daily Planner, those days containing activities are displayed in the Calendar with a red border, and free days are shown with no border. Double-click on a date to open the Daily Planner so you can enter new information or review existing information.

See also Daily Planner.

CAT AND MOUSE

In the Cat and Mouse game, a cat chases your mouse around the screen; when you move your mouse, the cat follows until you stop. When you stop moving the mouse, the cat goes to sleep until you move it again. You can change the Play Time, Speed, and Step sliders to change how the cat reacts on the screen. Select Register to save your current settings for future use.

CLIPBOARD VIEWER

The Clipboard Viewer lets you look at the contents of the clipboard, the area of temporary storage used in a cut, copy, or paste operation.

When Private Clipboard is selected from the Options menu, the information on the clipboard is available only to Presentation Manager applications. If you have to exchange information between the OS/2 and WIN-OS/2 clipboards, you must use the import and export options in the File menu.

If the clipboard is set to public, information can be shared between the two clipboards. The public clipboard choice must be selected in both clipboards.

DAILY PLANNER

You can use the Daily Planner to keep track of your activities, and you can store this information in a Daily Planner File. The Daily Planner file-name extension is .D. This file can be loaded by several of the other time-management applications on the desktop, including the Calendar, the Monthly Planner, and the Activities List.

Activities can be grouped according to type, and can include the built-in designations of Out-of-Office, Personal Holiday, or National Holiday. You can also add a graphic to the Activity Description box to jog your memory, or choose an alarm tune from a selection of built-in tunes. If you have a regularly occurring activity, use the Propagate/Delete Lines option from the Edit menu to automatically schedule the activity for you, rather than entering the event manually every time you want to schedule it. This feature is good for regularly scheduled events like softball games or department meetings.

As you mark events as completed using commands from the Completed menu, you can add them to your archive; any previously archived activity can be retrieved and restored to your Daily Planner schedule. The Tidy menu contains options you can use to delete and archive entries.

See also Activities List, Calendar, Monthly Planner, and Planner Archive.

DATABASE

The Database application supports a small, easy-to-use database, well-suited for use as an electronic or address book.

A Database file can hold up to 5000 records containing up to eight fields, and each field can contain up to 30 characters. In other words, the database can hold up to eight separate pieces of information on as many as 5000 people, as long as each piece of information is smaller than 30 letters or numbers. The Database also contains an *autodialer*, a feature that can dial a telephone number contained in the database.

To create a database from scratch, first choose New from the File menu, then use Edit Line Headings from the Edit menu to enter the names of the eight fields in the database. These fields might be Name, Address, City, State, Zip, Title, Phone, and Fax. Remember to save this information using the Save option from the File menu, then use Add a New Record from the Edit menu to add the appropriate entry information for all the people you want to keep in the database.

As you enter information into the database, the entry in the first field, "Name" in this example, is shown in the window to the right. If you want to review the information contained in a previously entered record, just double-click on the entry in this window. All the information will be displayed in the window on the left. Use the selections in the View menu to change from one field to another and to display database statistics.

To use the autodialer, you must have a modem attached to your computer. To set up the modem, use Dial Setup from the Customize menu. First select the port you will use with the modem, then enter any dialing or hangup information you want to use with the modem; see your modem manual for more information. To dial a number, locate the appropriate record in the database, then choose Dialing Function from the File menu. This collects all the numbers found in the record (including the address and the zip code) and displays them in a window. You choose the number that you want to dial and click on the Select button; after you know that the phone is ringing, press Enter and switch over to the telephone handset.

See also PM Terminal.

DATA UPDATE

The OS/2 version 2.0 Data Update application is the mechanism used to exchange information between OS/2 programs that support Dynamic Data Exchange (DDE). When information is exchanged between OS/2 programs, the exchange is considered to be *private*. To exchange information between an OS/2 application and a Windows program, you have to make the Data Update *public* using these steps:

1. Double-click on OS/2 System.
2. Double-click on Productivity.
3. Double-click on Data Update.

To make the exchange private once again, here are the steps:

1. Open the Window List using Ctrl+Esc.
2. Select Data Update.
3. Display the pop-up menu, and select Close.

ENHANCED EDITOR

The Enhanced Editor is a full-featured text editor, offering more features and capability than the OS/2 System Editor.

The File menu contains the usual options as well as a file import and a rename selection. The Edit menu supports the clipboard, as well as block or mark operations. The Search menu offers Find and

Find next options, as well as temporary and permanent book-marks. The Options menu lets you configure the operating details of the editor, and the Command menu gives you access to a command line so you can enter OS/2 or DOS commands, macros, or editor commands.

The Quick Reference option in the Help menu lists all the editing keystrokes and commands available in the Enhanced Editor. More importantly, you can add your own information or comments into this quick reference section using the Enhanced Editor. The quick reference file, EPMHELP.QHL, is located in the C:\OS2\APPS directory.

See also OS/2 System Editor.

FAX/PM

Fax/PM is a set of OS/2 version 2.1 fax management utilities that let you send and receive single-page faxes directly from the desktop. When you double-click Fax/PM inside the Productivity folder, you will see three objects:

- Fax/PM Scheduler lets you transmit and receive faxes and set up communications parameters.

- Fax/PM Viewer allows you to look at faxes that have been sent or received using Fax/PM; you can also copy all or part of a fax to the clipboard.

- Fax/PM DDE is a Fax/PM dynamic data exchange (DDE) server for Win-OS/2. You must start Fax/PM DDE before you try to send a fax from a WIN OS/2 program.

To configure Fax/PM, double-click on the Fax/PM Scheduler and select Setup from the Communications menu, or click on the setup icon at the top of the main window. This opens the four-page Fax/PM settings notebook:

- Communications lets you select the local communications port, dialing method, and modem for use with your fax.

- Miscellaneous allows you to enter sender identification information, select whether faxes are kept or deleted after they have been sent, and specify any necessary modem initialization commands.

- Receive lets you specify fax receive options: Auto Receive to make Fax/PM wait for incoming fax transmissions, the number of rings to wait before the modem answers, and path information for storing incoming faxes.

- Modem Tuning allows you to set the scan time, specify that a fax transmission begins with the first received XON character, or reverse the bit order used in the transmission.

To send a fax, double-click on the Fax/PM Scheduler, then select Requests from the Files menu, or click on the globe icon at the top left of the window. When the Send Requests window opens, double-click on the New field to enable the Create button. Now you can enter all the information relevant to this new fax, including the name of the document or file you want to fax, the document format, the destination fax number, and the Request State—choose between Ready (R) or Held (H).

You will also see information in the Request Selection List for faxes currently being processed by Fax/PM, including a Request sequence number; the destination fax number; the fax status, either R (Ready) for a fax that is waiting to be sent or H (Held) for a fax placed on hold; as well as the full path information for the document to be faxed. To change any of this information for an existing fax, double-click on the entry in the Request Selection List, then use the Modify or Delete buttons as appropriate. To abort a fax actually in the process of being sent, use the Stop Transmission option from the Communications menu.

You can also send a fax from within an application program. Just drag and drop the fax onto the Fax/PM icon on the desktop. A dialog box opens for you to enter the destination fax machine's telephone number.

Fax/PM Viewer lets you look at faxes you have sent or received with Fax/PM. Items in the Views menu help you specify how much of the fax you want to look at. If you plan to use the same view for every fax, make this choice in the Setup window. You can use the Edit menu to copy the fax to the clipboard, but you must use the large view to do so; the Select command in the Edit menu is not available in the other views.

ICON EDITOR

Desktop icons are one of the most useful and attractive elements in the OS/2 graphical user interface. Icons can represent application programs, groups of programs, or file folders. The Icon Editor lets you look at or change an icon, bit map, or pointer.

If you have used any of the popular paint programs, using the Icon Editor will be a breeze. Even if you haven't, it won't take you long to get the hang of it.

When you first open the Icon Editor, the workspace in the center of the window is blank. You can begin to create a new icon right away or you can load the icon file that you want to modify using the commands in the File menu. Icon files have the file-name extension .ICO. Each icon is defined as a square element, 32 pixels (picture elements) wide by 32 pixels high. Each of these pixels is equivalent to one spot of color in an icon. The small square at the top left of the window displays the icon at its actual size. You can also assign a color to each of the two mouse buttons, and these colors are displayed on the replica mouse next to the icon display.

The Edit menu contains the usual options, as well as commands to flip a shape horizontally or vertically. The Palette menu helps you work with different color sets, and the Options menu controls Editor-wide settings, as well as pen-size selections. The Device menu contains advanced display device selections. The Tools menu helps you to identify the colors in an icon; and its Color Fill command floods a shape with the color assigned to a mouse button.

JIGSAW

The Jigsaw game makes a jigsaw puzzle from a graphical image. Select the image you want to use in the Open option in the File menu, then choose how large you want to make the pieces using

Size from the Options menu. When you are ready to play, select Jumble! from the Options menu. Now use the mouse to put the pieces back together again.

MONTHLY PLANNER

The Monthly Planner gives you a monthly perspective on your activities. You can open a file created with the Daily Planner and show the information in the Monthly Planner format. The Daily Planner file-name extension is .D.

Available time is shown in white, and scheduled activities are shown in contrasting colors. Weekends are shown in gray, and any days displayed from the previous or following months are shown in a different shade of gray.

An alarm is represented by a red dot in the lower corner of the activity. The first two letters of the activity description are also shown, so if you can, establish a set of two-letter codes to represent the different activities you want to track, and you will be able to see them in this monthly view. If you use a graphic as the first character of an activity, it will be displayed instead.

To see all the details of an activity, double-click anywhere on the bar representing the day you are interested in, and the Daily Planner will open so you can review, edit, or delete the information.

See also Daily Planner.

NOTEPAD

The Notepad contains a set of five pages you can use to collect short notes and reminders. The Notepad is not a word processor, but it is very useful for jotting down thoughts and ideas you don't want to forget.

Each of the five pages can contain up to 25 lines of information, and each line can be up to 180 characters in length. The usual menu selections in the File menu help you to open and save Notepad files; Notepad files have the file-name extension .N.

The five pages of the Notepad are shown cascaded across the screen; to switch between pages, just click on the page you want to bring to the front. You can also use the selections in the View menu to manage the pages. The selections in the Edit menu help you manage the Notepad and provide a way of adding graphical characters to your notes, while the Customize menu controls colors and font sizes.

See also Sticky Pad.

OS/2 CHESS

The chess game works like the traditional board game, and you can play against the computer or against other human players on your network. You can take advantage of a surprising number of options, including a move timer, sounds, and warning messages. You can even turn the board round when it is time for your move.

OS/2 SYSTEM EDITOR

The OS/2 System Editor is the text editor that was included with previous versions of OS/2. It offers basic text manipulation features, along with clipboard support, font and color selections, a find and replace option, and word wrap. The OS/2 System Editor is used to review or change OS/2 system text files, such as CONFIG.SYS or README, and it is the default editor used by the Seek and Scan Files application. If you need more from a text editor, use the Enhanced Editor instead.

See also Enhanced Editor, Seek and Scan Files.

PICTURE VIEWER

The Picture Viewer lets you look at three different kinds of files: metafiles, picture interchange files, and spool files.

A *metafile* is a special kind of graphics file that contains not only the image, but also instructions on how the image should be displayed. This allows the image to be output to a variety of different display devices. Metafiles always have the file-name extension .MET.

A *picture interchange file* is a special file format used in exchanging images between applications. Picture interchange files always have the file-name extension .PIC. Use the Code Page selection from the Options menu to select a code page for the country of origin of the file, if the file was created elsewhere. A code page is just a collection of letters and numbers, but you need the right one to make sense of the displayed information.

A *spool file* contains information that is waiting to be printed. Spool files have the file-name extension .SPL. You can display some of the information in a spool file, as long as the file contains a picture in the standard OS/2 format.

Use the Open option from the File menu to specify the type of file you want to view. The Edit menu contains the normal selections, and the Page menu helps you to move though the information you display, page by page. The Options menu contains Viewer-wide control selections, while the Sequence menu works to show information as part of a series of images.

PLANNER ARCHIVE

The Planner Archive maintains the information you saved from the Daily Planner using the options in the Completed and Tidy menus. This information is stored in a separate file you can open and review with the Planner Archive. The Planner Archive file-name extension is .$DA.

The Statistics option from the File menu lets you review your activities with a time breakdown over a specific month. You can also sort archived activities using up to three different sort fields.

Note that activities erased from the Daily Planner are not available to the Planner Archive; only those activities you archived are available.

See also Daily Planner.

PM CHART

PM Chart is a business graphics application you can use to create charts and graphs. This program can open and display files created by Micrografx Charisma either as a graphic (.GRF) or as data (.DAT), and it can open and display Micrografx Draw files (DRW). It can also import data from files using the following formats: data interchange format (.DIF), space-delimited ASCII (.SPC), Microsoft symbolic link (.SLK), Lotus 1-2-3 (.WK1 and .WKS), and Microsoft Excel (.XLS). You can also create a brand new file using PM Chart. Choose the appropriate file type in the Open selection in the File menu. PM Chart can save files in either .GRF or in .DRW file formats.

The tool bar shown down the left side of the work area contains the following tools, from top to bottom:

- Select arrow. This option turns off the previous mode.

- Create or edit a worksheet. The worksheet can hold up to 100 rows and 75 columns of information. When you are in worksheet mode, you can use the Data menu to sort the worksheet or to apply simple arithmetic functions. You can also specify a constant for use with these functions.

- View a symbol. Choose the view level or zoom mode.

- Draw a symbol. Select one of the drawing functions to create a rectangle, curve, ellipse, straight line, and so on.

- Create a chart. Choose from area, bar, column, line, pie, exploded pie, or table chart. Three-dimensional effects are also supported.

- Type text. Create a text object to annotate a chart, select the font and type style, and choose the text-justification options you want to use.

- Change colors and style of fill, line and text.

The Edit menu provides options for cut-and-paste operations, and for clearing and removing objects from the workspace.

The Change and Preferences menus appear and disappear automatically as you move in and out of worksheet mode. The Change menu lets you modify a selected symbol or group of symbols, and the Preferences menu lets you specify the default values to use when drawing figures.

To create a chart from scratch, follow these steps:

1. Enter the data into the worksheet, either by hand or by loading one of the approved file types. Note that PM Chart cannot load files created by the Spreadsheet.

2. Select the data in the worksheet that you want to include in the chart by pressing the left mouse button and dragging the pointer over the desired area.

3. Choose the chart type you want to use from the selections available from the tool bar.

4. Use New to create the selected chart, Overlay to combine charts, Replace to delete the selected chart and replace it with a new one, or Cancel to return to the workspace.

You can also choose among several optional items: 3D creates a three-dimensional image, Legend adds a small legend to the chart, or New positions the chart in the center of the workspace.

After creating the chart, you can change its shape by dragging one of the black handles, or *control points*, to a new location. You can also add text labels or titles to your chart in a variety of fonts or type styles. Use the options in the File menu to save your chart when it is complete.

See also Spreadsheet.

PM TERMINAL

PM Terminal (Softerm) is full-featured communications and terminal-emulation program for use with a modem over telephone lines. PM Terminal has two main modes, the Session Manager and the Session Window.

The Session Manager establishes and maintains communications information and collects all this information into profiles which are saved on disk in a file called CUSTOM.MDB. Each profile contains all the information needed to start and then manage a communications session with one specific target system, including terminal emulation information, environment information, connection and modem information, file-transfer protocol selections, and telephone numbers. Several online service templates are shown in the opening PM Terminal screen. Double-click on one of these templates to enter your own local configuration data for the service.

The Session Window, also known as the Runtime window, Terminal Emulation window, or Online window, orchestrates your online transactions using information from one of the profiles you established in the Session Manager. When you are online, you will be in one of the following modes of operation:

- Terminal Emulation mode. This mode turns your computer into a terminal and is most often used for communications with a large remote computer. PM Terminal supports all the popular terminal types you are ever likely to need.

- File Transfer mode. In this mode you can exchange files with a remote computer using a pre-established file-transfer protocol. PM Terminal supports all the popular file-transfer protocols, including Xmodem, Ymodem, and KERMIT.

Once you are online, you will see a new set of menus at the top of the window that give you control over the current operation, including options for file transfer or display, dialing a number, hanging up the modem, and transferring files to disk or to a printer. A status line at the bottom of this window indicates you are online and contains other status information, depending on which mode you are using.

PM Terminal is a complex and flexible application capable of meeting all your computer-to-computer communications needs.

PULSE

The Pulse application shows a small graph of the activity of your computer's microprocessor. The higher the graph, the more work your computer is doing. The graph is updated continuously, so you can see the effects of opening and closing applications.

You can also use Pulse to monitor the activity level of a program or system utility running in the background. As a demonstration, start formatting a floppy disk, then return to the desktop and run Pulse. You might be surprised at the low level of activity; you can see that your computer is not doing very much work as it formats the disk.

The selections in the Options menu let you control the display colors and the nature of the graph. You can even freeze the graph to capture an important event if you wish.

REVERSI

Reversi works just like the board game of the same name. The objective is to have more red pieces on the board at the end of the game than the computer has blue pieces. The game is over when all the squares on the board are filled, or when no more legal moves can be made.

SCRAMBLE

The Scramble game is the same as the hand-held version of this game; the objective is to unscramble the numbers.

SEEK AND SCAN FILES

The Seek and Scan Files application (also known as PMSeek) can find a lost or misplaced file anywhere in your directory structure on any drive. It can also find specific text inside the files you are looking for.

There are just a few steps involved in using Seek and Scan Files:

1. Tell Seek and Scan Files *what* to look for by entering a file name in the File Name to Search For box.

2. Tell Seek and Scan Files *where* to look using the Drives to Search check boxes.

3. Tell Seek and Scan Files about any text you are looking for.

4. Start the search by selecting the Search button.

When Seek and Scan Files locates files that match your specified settings, they are listed in the Files Found box in the lower half of the window. The information displayed for each file includes its complete path, the file date and time, and the file size. Use Stop to halt the search, and use Open to open the default text editor on the file so you can review its contents. If the Enhanced Editor is iconized on the desktop, you can drag and drop a file onto its icon, and the Enhanced Editor will open the file.

After selecting a file in the Files Found box, you can use the options from the Selected menu to open the default editor on the file, to run the located program file, or to execute an operating system command such as REN or DEL on the located file.

With settings from the Options menu, you can extend the search to include subdirectories, make the text search case sensitive or case insensitive, display the found text, and clear the Files Found box when you initiate a new search.

SOLITAIRE

The Solitaire game is just like the card game. And yes, you can still cheat; see the selections in the Moves menu.

SPREADSHEET

The Spreadsheet application creates a simple 26-column by 80-row spreadsheet you can use to keep track of expenses, sales figures, or other numbers.

Spreadsheet is no match for the high-powered spreadsheets from the major software companies, but how often do you need all that power? You will be surprised how well Spreadsheet performs.

To create a new spreadsheet:

1. Select New from the File menu.

2. Enter the numbers into the Spreadsheet.

3. Use Save or Save As from the File menu to save the contents of the Spreadsheet.

You can use all the major operators—addition (+), subtraction (–), multiplication (*), and division (/)—to add simple formulas to your spreadsheet. You can sum or add all the cells in a range of cells with the area summation (@), and you can use square brackets ([]) to change the order in which a calculation is performed. Adding titles above your entries is a good way to make the spreadsheet more readable.

Use the options in the Recalculate menu to establish just when and how you want the spreadsheet recalculated. If your spreadsheet is large, it will be faster to recalculate only those cells that have changed, rather than recalculate the whole worksheet.

When it is time to print your spreadsheet, use the Print selection from the File menu. To see the formulas in your spreadsheet, use the Print Formula/Cell Data option instead.

STICKY PAD

The Sticky Pad application lets you stick notes on objects on your desktop.

You can create up to ten notes, and each one can contain up to eight lines of 29 characters or graphical elements. As soon as you type a character into a note, a timestamp appears on the first line of the note. You can use the Reset Timestamp option from the Edit menu to change this if you wish.

Here are the steps to follow when creating a new note:

1. Open the Sticky Pad icon.

2. Drag the sticky note into the target window and drop it.

3. Type the note.

4. When you minimize the window, the sticky note will be attached to that window, and when the window is displayed, the note will appear in one of the corners.

5. As long as the Sticky Pad remains open, the note will remain attached to the window. If you close the Sticky Pad, the note will disappear.

The selections in the Customize menu help you to place the note in the right position. You can also drag the note using the mouse.

TO-DO LIST

The To-Do List lets you organize the things you have to do, assign them a priority, and store them in a file. The To-Do List file-name extension is .T.

You can enter a two-character priority into the Priority column, a date into the Date column, and a brief description into the Task-Description column. Using the Sort option from the View menu, you can sort by priority, date, or description to arrange your tasks into the order you want. If you use a graphic element as the priority indicator, note that graphics are sorted to the end of the list, after numbers and letters.

Use the selections from the Mark menu to show that tasks are complete. The word *Done* appears in the Priority column opposite the appropriate entry.

The To-Do List has its own archive, called the To-Do List Archive, because the To-Do List is not one of the group of applications that use Daily Planner information. Use the options from the Mark menu to archive or delete completed tasks.

See also To-Do List Archive.

TO-DO LIST ARCHIVE

The To-Do List Archive maintains the information you saved from the To-Do List using the options in the Mark menu. This information is stored in a separate file you can open and review with the To-Do List Archive. The To-Do List Archive file-name extension is .$TA.

You can sort archived activities using up to four different sort fields, including priority, date, description, or archive date.

Note that activities erased from the To-Do List are not available in the To-Do List Archive; only those activities you archived are available.

See also To-Do List.

TUNE EDITOR

The Tune Editor can display, create, or change the tunes used with the Alarms application.

Each tune file can contain up to 36 individual tunes, and each tune can contain up to 20 different notes. Use the Open option in the File menu to open the default tune file PMDIARY.$$A; this file contains the tunes used by the Alarm application. Now use the Open Tune selection to choose the tune you want to display in the Tune Editor window. The Play menu lets you play either the current tune, or cycle through all the tunes contained in the current tune file.

If you want to edit the current tune, use the selections from the Edit menu to add sharps or flats, or change the timing value of a note in the tune. You can also use the value, note, pitch, and tempo sliders to make changes in a tune.

These tunes do not require any special hardware; they use the normal computer speaker to generate their tones.

Part IV

Running OS/2, DOS, and Windows Programs under OS/2

In many ways, OS/2 offers the best of all possible worlds: you can run OS/2 applications, DOS applications, and Microsoft Windows applications, and you can run them without changing anything in your system setup. You can run these applications in side-by-side windows on the desktop, or you can run them as full-screen sessions if that is more convenient.

RUNNING OS/2 PROGRAMS

Running OS/2 programs is easy once you understand how to use the desktop. To start a program, just double-click on the folder that contains the application, then double-click on the appropriate icon to start the application running.

OS/2 applications can take advantage of several important operating system features:

- Multitasking. This is the ability to run several programs on your computer at the same time. Multitasking allows you to format a floppy disk, download a file from an online information service or bulletin board, or update a large database, all at the same time that you are working on a letter in your word processor.

- Crash protection. OS/2 protects applications from each other, so that if one program has a problem it does not bring down the whole operating system. You just have to restart the application that had the problem.

- Larger memory. OS/2 removes the 640K memory limitation so familiar to MS-DOS users, as well as removing the need for a separate memory-management program. OS/2 takes care of everything.

- Dynamic Data Exchange. A productivity application, Data Update, helps you exchange data between running OS/2 programs, or between OS/2 and Windows.

- Graphical User Interface (GUI). The graphical user interface, or workplace shell, has a strong object-oriented design where almost everything is treated as an object, including icons, folders, applications, and files.

- High Performance File System (HPFS). The HPFS is a file-management system unique to OS/2. It offers better file-naming features, faster disk access, and up to 64K of extended attributes per file.

OS/2 programs can be set up to run in an OS/2 window or as an OS/2 full screen.

In rest of this section, we'll look at running MS-DOS and Windows programs under OS/2.

DOS AND WINDOWS PROGRAMS UNDER OS/2

OS/2 runs MS-DOS programs by *emulating* MS-DOS; in other words, a part of the OS/2 operating system software looks and works just like MS-DOS. For most purposes, this emulation is complete, but there are some programs in the following categories that may refuse to run:

- Certain games programs.

- Some communications programs.

- Many diagnostic utilities. Programs like the Norton Disk Doctor from Symantec or DiskFix from Central Point Software will politely refuse to run in a multitasking environment. Other programs may not be as well behaved, so be careful.

You might need a specific version of MS-DOS to run a particular program that does not run well under OS/2's DOS emulation. If you have a bootable floppy disk containing the right version of MS-DOS, you can use the object called DOS from Drive A to start this version as a separate DOS session. Alternatively, you can run the program from an extended MS-DOS partition on drive C. Finally, you can run MS-DOS from your hard disk using an *image file*; see the VMDISK entry in Part V, "OS/2 Commands," for more information.

OS/2 also contains software to emulate, or mimic, Microsoft Windows, so you do not have to buy a copy to run your Windows applications programs. If you already had a copy of Microsoft Windows installed on your hard disk before you installed OS/2, you might consider removing it (but not your Windows application programs) to save hard disk space.

OS/2 refers to these emulations as a *DOS session* or a *WIN-OS/2 session*, respectively.

RUNNING DOS PROGRAMS FROM THE DESKTOP

To run an MS-DOS program from the desktop, follow these steps:

1. Open the folder that contains your MS-DOS programs.

2. Double-click on the icon that represents the program you want to run.

When you quit the program, you will return to the desktop. You can also return to the desktop by opening the Window List with Ctrl+Esc. If you do this, you will notice that the name of the application you were working with is shown as an entry in the Window List. You can double-click on the entry to return to the session.

RUNNING DOS PROGRAMS FROM THE DOS-SESSION PROMPT

If you need to work at the DOS system prompt, follow these steps:

1. Double-click on the OS/2 System icon on the desktop.

2. Double-click on the Command Prompts folder.

3. Now you can choose to run DOS as a window on the desktop by selecting the DOS Window icon, or as a full-screen session by selecting the DOS Full Screen icon.

Now type the DOS commands you want to use directly at the DOS command prompt. See Part V, "OS/2 Commands," for a description of the commands available from the DOS prompt.

You can also use the steps above to start a DOS application for which there is no OS/2 desktop icon. When you quit the application, you return to the DOS session, not directly to the OS/2 desktop. You can use Ctrl+Esc to return to the desktop, and you can use the Window List to go from the desktop back to the DOS session. The entries in the Window List will be DOS Window and DOS Full Screen, respectively.

To close the DOS window, double-click on the icon in the top left corner of the title bar.

STARTING WINDOWS PROGRAMS UNDER OS/2

Using OS/2, you can run a Windows application in the following ways:

- As a full-screen application where the Windows program takes over the whole screen. This is the default mode.

- In an OS/2 window on the desktop. You can only run one WIN- OS/2 window session at a time, but that session can handle several Windows applications.

- In an OS/2 window, but as a separate WIN-OS/2 session. To use this option, you must change the program settings as described under the heading "Changing Session Settings" later in this section before you start running the application.

There are several different methods you can use to start your Windows applications:

- From the OS/2 desktop. As with all applications, this is the preferred method. Double-click on the folder that contains your Windows applications, then double-click on the icon for the program you want to run. When you quit the program, you return to the desktop.

- From the Windows desktop. Double-click on the OS/2 System icon on the desktop, then double-click on the Command Prompts folder, and finally, double-click on the WIN-OS/2 Full Screen icon. The Program Manager window opens, and you can use all of the usual Windows features. To return to the OS/2 desktop, choose Exit WIN-OS/2 selection from the Program Manager File menu, select Close from the system menu, or double-click on the close box to return to the OS/2 desktop when you are done. Closing the session automatically exits each running Windows program.

• From the OS/2 or DOS command prompt. Type **WINOS2** followed by path and file-name information at the command prompt. For example, to run Microsoft Word for Windows from the OS/2 session prompt, type

WINOS2 C:\WINWORD\WINWORD.EXE

When you quit the program, you return to the command prompt, not the desktop.

To return to the OS/2 desktop without closing your Windows session, select the OS/2 Desktop icon at the bottom of the WIN-OS/2 session screen. Select the program or session name from the Window List to return to your WIN-OS/2 session.

STARTING WINDOWS PROGRAMS AUTOMATICALLY

You can set up a WIN-OS/2 session so that it automatically starts one or more Windows programs. Follow these steps:

1. Select the Command Prompts folder from the OS/2 System icon.

2. Open the pop-up menu for WIN-OS/2 Full Screen, then select the arrow to the right of the Open command.

3. Select Settings, then select Program.

4. In the Parameters field, type the path and file-name information for each program you want to start automatically, separating each one with commas. Add an exclamation point (!) before a file name if you want the application to appear as an icon when the session begins.

5. Close the Program Settings window.

Next time you start a Windows session, your chosen application will start automatically. When you close the application, you return directly to the OS/2 desktop once again.

CHANGING SESSION SETTINGS

There are many settings you can use to "tune" your OS/2, DOS, or Windows sessions. They fall into the following groups:

• Memory configuration

• Keyboard support

• Mouse and touch-screen support

• Ctrl+Break support

• Program speed

• Video support

• Communications parameters

• Printer functions

To look at or change any of these settings, follow these steps:

1. Display the pop-up menu for the object whose setting you want to change by clicking the right mouse button on its icon.

2. Click on the arrow to the right of the Open command, then select Settings.

3. Select Session, then choose the type of session from OS/2 Full Screen, OS/2 Window, DOS Full Screen, DOS Window, WIN-OS Full Screen, and WIN-OS Window. You can also choose Separate Session for a WIN-OS/2 session; see the heading "Starting Windows Programs under OS/2" earlier in this section for more details.

4. Select the setting you want to look at or change from the list. It is a good idea to note the setting's original value, so you can reset it if you wish.

5. Select Save to keep your changes.

Many of the DOS and WIN-OS/2 settings can only be changed before you start a session; if you change them during a session, your changes may not be saved for future sessions.

Part V

OS/2 Commands

This section lists all the OS/2 commands in alphabetical order, and includes a command description, a syntax and description for each command, as well as examples and special usage notes when appropriate. For users migrating to OS/2 from MS-DOS 5, these notes will also draw your attention to any significant differences between an OS/2 DOS session command and the equivalent command in MS-DOS 5.

Most of the commands listed in this section are available in both OS/2 sessions and in DOS sessions, although some are specific to one operating system or the other. To indicate usage, you will see the following icons throughout this section.

 This icon indicates that the command is only available in an OS/2 session.

 This icon indicates that the command is only available in a DOS session.

If a command is available in both OS/2 and in DOS sessions, you will see both icons shown side by side.

These icons are also used in Part VI, "CONFIG.SYS Commands," and Part VII, " Batch File Commands."

In the syntax descriptions, required parameters are shown in *bold italic*, while optional parameters are shown in *italic*.

ANSI

OS/2

ANSI enables or disables extended display and keyboard support
for OS/2 programs; most OS/2 programs do not need this special
support.

• SYNTAX AND DESCRIPTION

ANSI *ON*
ANSI *OFF*

ANSI enables or disables the processing of ANSI control sequences
in an OS/2 session. ANSI control sequences usually begin with an
escape character, and they are used to redefine keys on the keyboard, control the cursor, or change the display color attributes.

If you use this command without a parameter, the current ANSI
status is displayed.

Specify ANSI ON to enable extended display and keyboard support. This is also the default setting.

Specify ANSI OFF to disable this support.

• NOTES   The KEYS ON command, used to control and edit the
command line, always disables ANSI extended keyboard support.

See also DEVICE in Part VI, "CONFIG.SYS Commands," and
KEYS, later in this section.

APPEND

APPEND tells DOS programs where to find data files that are not in the current directory. APPEND is similar to the PATH command, except that the PATH command refers to runnable files only, while the APPEND command refers to all files.

• SYNTAX AND DESCRIPTION

APPEND *dir1*; *dir2*; */switches*

APPEND can be used from the command line, or it can be added to your AUTOEXEC.BAT file. The first time you use APPEND, it acts as an OS/2 external command, and you may have to specify drive and path information to locate the command. After APPEND is loaded, it becomes an internal command; the drive and path information are no longer needed. You can append as many directories as you can specify in 128 characters.

• SWITCHES

dir1; *dir2*	Specifies the drives and directories to be appended. You can specify more than one directory; separate them by a semicolon.
/PATH:ON	Allows APPEND to search for data files that include drive or path or both drive and path in their names. This is the default setting.
/PATH:OFF	Prevents APPEND from searching for data files that include both drive and/or path in their names. If you use /PATH:OFF and then type a drive or a path, APPEND will not search for the file; if you type just the file name, APPEND will find the file.

/E   Stores the specified search path in the
                            OS/2 environment space, so that the
                            information can be accessed by other
                            application programs. You can only use /E
                            the first time you use APPEND in a DOS
                            session.

If you use this command without a parameter, the current AP-
PEND directory list is displayed on the screen.

• EXAMPLES

To tell all DOS programs to look for data files in the C:\FILES directory and the D:\DATA directory, type

APPEND C:\FILES;D:\DATA

To display the current APPEND settings on the screen, type

APPEND

If you type

APPEND;

you cancel the current APPEND setting.

• NOTES   In an OS/2 DOS session, APPEND does not include
the MS-DOS 5 /X:ON or /X:OFF switches.

See also DPATH, PATH. Both these commands are detailed in Part VI,
"CONFIG.SYS Commands."

ASSIGN

ASSIGN redirects disk operations to a drive other than the specified drive. This command is most often used with older application programs that only use drives A and B; ASSIGN does not work on a hard disk.

• SYNTAX AND DESCRIPTION

ASSIGN *drive1 = drive2 /switches*

With the ASSIGN command, *drive1* specifies the drive that will not be used when ASSIGN is in effect; all references to this drive are redirected to *drive2*. *drive2* specifies the drive that will be used when ASSIGN is in effect; all references to *drive1* are sent to this drive. Do not include a colon with either drive letter.

• SWITCHES

/S   Displays the current drive reassignments.

• EXAMPLES

To assign all requests for drive B to drive C, type

ASSIGN B=C

or .

ASSIGN B C

The equals sign may be replaced by a space.

If you want to see if drive assignments are active, type

ASSIGN /S

To reset all drives back to their original assignments, use ASSIGN with no switches.

• NOTES When ASSIGN is in effect, the following commands do not work on the drive where ASSIGN is active: CHKDSK, DISKCOMP, DISKCOPY, FORMAT, JOIN, LABEL, PRINT, RECOVER, RESTORE, SUBST.

The /S switch lists the same drive reassignment information that the MS-DOS 5 /STATUS switch provides.

ATTRIB

OS/2 DOS

The ATTRIB command displays or changes a file's attributes.

• SYNTAX AND DESCRIPTION

ATTRIB *mode* ***filename*** */switches*

With the ATTRIB command, *filename* specifies the file or file names whose attributes will be changed. The *filename* may include drive and path information, as well as wildcard characters; all the file names matching the *filename* specification will be changed.

ATTRIB lets you look at or change four attributes:

Read-Only (R)	A read-only file cannot be modified or deleted by the normal file-management commands.
Archive (A)	This attribute tells the BACKUP or XCOPY commands that the file should be included in the next backup operation. This attribute is set and cleared, as appropriate, automatically by the operating system.

| System (S) | This attribute indicates that this file is a system file. It is also hidden, and cannot be accessed by most other operating system commands. |
| Hidden (H) | When this attribute is set, the file becomes invisible to most of the file-manipulation commands. |

The *mode* parameter tells the ATTRIB command whether to set or reset each attribute, as follows:

+A	Turns on the archive attribute.
-A	Turns off the archive attribute.
+H	Turns on the hidden attribute, making the file into a hidden file that is not shown in directory listings.
-H	Turns off the hidden attribute, making the file appear in directory listings once again.
+R	Sets the read-only bit.
-R	Turns off, or resets, the read-only bit.
+S	Turns on the system attribute.
-S	Resets the system attribute.

• SWITCHES

/S   Includes all files that match the *filename* parameter in subdirectories. This is especially useful if the same file exists in several different directories and you want to change an attribute on all copies of the file.

• EXAMPLES

To turn on the archive attribute of a file called MEMO.TXT, type the following:

ATTRIB +A MEMO.TXT

To turn off the archive attribute on MEMO.TXT, type

ATTRIB -A MEMO.TXT

If you want to make MEMO.TXT into a read-only file, type

ATTRIB +R MEMO.TXT

and to turn it back into a normal file, type

ATTRIB -R MEMO.TXT

If you use the command without a *mode* parameter, ATTRIB displays the attributes of all the files matching the *filename* parameter. Use

ATTRIB ATTRIB.EXE

to see a list of the attribute settings for this particular file, or type

ATTRIB C:*.* /S

if you want to see a list of the current attributes for all files on drive C.

● **NOTES**   A file can have one or more attributes set at any given time, or, alternatively, it may have none of its attributes set.

See also BACKUP, RESTORE, XCOPY.

BACKUP

The BACKUP command copies files from one disk to another using a special file format to optimize the use of space on the backup disk. The BACKUP command is an insurance policy against hard disk failure and the resulting loss of information. Back up your system regularly; be prepared.

You can also use BACKUP and the companion command, RESTORE, to move a file or set of files from one computer to another.

• SYNTAX AND DESCRIPTION

BACKUP *source: target:* /*switches*

You must specify both *source* and *target* for the BACKUP command. The *source* drive is the drive that contains the files that you want to back up, usually a hard disk, while the *target* drive is the drive to which all the files will be copied, usually a floppy disk. As a minimum, *source* and *target* must specify unique drive letters (you cannot use the same drive letter for both), and *source* can also include path information, file names, or wildcard characters.

When the BACKUP command fills a floppy disk but there are still files waiting to be backed up, BACKUP asks you to insert another disk. Label and number the floppy disks with the date and the disk number in sequence as they are created by the BACKUP command. If you have to use the RESTORE command later, you will be asked to load the disks in the same order.

BACKUP does not back up the OS/2 system files (CMD.EXE and COMMAND.COM), hidden system files, or any open dynamic data link (DLL) files; you will see an error message from BACKUP if you try to back up these files.

The OS/2 HPFS allows up to 64K of extended attributes to be associated with each file or directory. These extended attributes are maintained by application programs and can include notes, comments, and information about icons. The BACKUP command will automatically back up all extended attributes along with the appropriate file. The ATTRIB command cannot display or change these extended attributes.

• SWITCHES

/A   Adds the new files to the end of an existing backup disk. When you use BACKUP with this switch, existing backup files are not erased or overwritten by the new files.

/D:*mm-dd-yy* Backs up only those files created or modified after the specified date. This switch is usually used with the /T switch. The date must be entered in the appropriate form specified by the COUNTRY command in your CONFIG.SYS file. See Part VI for more information on CONFIG.SYS and COUNTRY.

/F:*nnn* Formats an unformatted target floppy disk before backing files up to the disk. This switch cannot be used on hard disks, and will not format a previously formatted floppy disk. By specifying this switch, you do not have to know the exact number of disks needed for the backup before you begin; you can format new disks as required. Specify *nnn* to define the size of the floppy disk in kilobytes, as follows:

 360 = 360K double-sided 5.25"

 720 = 720K double-sided 3.5"

 1200 = 1.2MB double-sided 5.25"

 1440 = 1.44MB high-density 3.5"

 2880 = 2.88MB high-density 3.5"

/L:*filename* Creates a backup log file with the specified file name. If no file name is specified, the default file BACKUP.LOG is created in the root directory of the source drive. This log file contains information about all the files backed up during the current backup.

/M Backs up only the files that have been created or changed since the last backup operation was performed.

/S Includes files contained in subdirectories below the current directory in the backup.

/T:*hh:mm:ss*   Backs up only those files created or mod-
                       ified after the specified time. You can use the
                       /D and the /T switches together to define
                       exactly the files you want to back up.

• EXAMPLES

To back up all the files in the root directory of drive C to a floppy
disk in drive A, type

BACKUP C: A:

To make sure files in subdirectories are also included in the backup,
type

BACKUP C: A: /S

If you just want to back up a single file, type

BACKUP C:\MYSTUFF \MYFILE.TXT A:

If you want to back up files created on or after January 1993, type

BACKUP C: A: /D:01-01-93

To back up all the files and subdirectories on drive C to drive A
without overwriting any previous backup, formatting any new
1.44MB 3.5" disks as needed, type

BACKUP C:*.* A: /A /S /F:1440

• **NOTES**   The BACKUP command cannot be run in a DOS session;
you will see a message to this effect if you try to run the command.

See also ATTRIB, RESTORE, XCOPY.

BOOT

The BOOT command switches between the OS/2 and the DOS operating systems when they are both installed on the same hard disk drive, drive C.

• SYNTAX AND DESCRIPTION

BOOT *switches*

The BOOT command is available from an OS/2 session command prompt, from an OS/2 DOS session command prompt, or from a DOS command prompt, and can be used if:

- A version of DOS later than version 3.2 (later versions of DOS are recommended for more complete OS/2 compatibility) was resident on drive C before OS/2 was installed.

- Drive C was not reformatted during the OS/2 installation.

- The HPFS was not installed on drive C.

Before running the BOOT command, be sure to complete all system operations and end all application programs, otherwise data may be lost.

• SWITCHES

/OS2   Changes to the OS/2 operating system from MS-DOS.

/DOS   Changes to the MS-DOS operating system from OS/2 or from an OS/2 DOS session.

• EXAMPLES

To change to MS-DOS from OS/2, type

BOOT /DOS

from either the OS/2 command prompt, or from the DOS prompt of an OS/2 DOS session.

If you want to switch to OS/2 from MS-DOS, type the following from the OS2 directory:

BOOT /OS2

• **NOTES**   When you turn your computer on, the operating system that was last running when you turned it off is automatically reloaded.

CD OR CHDIR

The CD command changes the current directory. CD is an abbreviation for the CHDIR command; you can use either because they both do the same thing.

• SYNTAX AND DESCRIPTION

CD *drive: path*

where *drive: path* specifies the location of the directory you want to change to.

You can use the CD command to change to a different directory on the current drive, change to a subdirectory of your current directory, go straight to the root directory, or change to the parent directory of your current directory.

If you use CD with no options, the name of the current directory is displayed.

• EXAMPLES

To change from your current directory to the OS2 directory, type

CD \OS2

To change to the SYSTEM subdirectory within the OS2 directory, type

CD SYSTEM

If you want to return back up your directory structure one directory at a time, type the following command several times; you change to the parent directory of your current directory every time you type it.

CD ..

The .. option is a shorthand way of specifying the name of the parent of your current directory. If you want to go straight from your current directory to the root directory, type the shorthand sequence:

**CD **

To display the name of your current directory, type the command without any options:

CD

• NOTES   See also DIR, MD, RD, TREE.

CHCP

The CHCP command lets you swap between two code-page character sets defined in your CONFIG.SYS startup file.

• SYNTAX AND DESCRIPTION

CHCP *nnn*

The *nnn* option is the number of the code page you want to change to.

As part of OS/2's international language support, each country supported by OS/2 has a unique country code, and each country code supports a primary code page and at least one alternative code page. A code page consists of 256 characters that your keyboard can generate, your screen can display, and your printer can print. Only one code page can be in use at a time.

These code pages determine the characters produced when you use the keyboard corresponding to the COUNTRY statement in your CONFIG.SYS file. See Part VI for more information on COUNTRY and CONFIG.SYS.

In the United States, OS/2 defaults to the following code pages:

437	United States
850	Multilingual

Many other code pages are available, including the following:

860	Portuguese
861	Icelandic
863	French Canadian
865	Norway
932	Japan
938	Republic of China

If you use the CHCP command with no options, you will see the number of the active code page displayed on the screen, along with the numbers of both the prepared system code pages.

• EXAMPLES

To change from code page 437 to code page 850, type

CHCP 850

To see the number of the current active code page, type

CHCP

• **NOTES**   See also the KEYB entry later in this section, and the CODEPAGE, COUNTRY, and DEVINFO entries in Part VI, "CON-FIG.SYS Commands."

CHKDSK

The CHKDSK command produces a status report on your files and directories. When used with the appropriate switch, CHKDSK can fix certain file-related problems. CHKDSK also displays the disk volume label and volume serial number.

• **SYNTAX AND DESCRIPTION**

CHKDSK *drive: path filename /switches*

If you use CHKDSK without parameters, you will analyze your current drive; specify a drive letter if you want to analyze a different drive. CHKDSK reports the following:

- The type of file system in use, FAT or HPFS
- The disk volume label
- The disk volume serial number
- The total formatted disk space, in bytes
- The amount of space occupied by hidden files, in bytes
- The number of hidden files
- The amount of space occupied by directories
- The number of directories

- The amount of space occupied by user files, in bytes
- The number of user files
- The amount of space occupied by extended attributes, in bytes
- The remaining available disk space, in bytes
- The size of the disk allocation unit, in bytes
- The total number of disk allocation units on the disk
- The number of available disk allocation units

If you run CHKDSK in a DOS session, you will also see:

- The total amount of conventional memory available to the DOS session, in bytes
- The conventional memory available for application programs, in bytes

CHKDSK can also fix certain disk errors known as lost clusters. These are parts of files that the operating system did not save properly for some reason; they are unusable as lost clusters and they occupy valuable disk space. If CHKDSK finds lost clusters on your disk, it asks if you want to convert them into files.

If you answer yes, CHKDSK converts the lost clusters into files so that you can examine their contents and delete them if they are not needed. The files created by CHKDSK are stored in the root directory of the disk and are named FILE*nnnn*.CHK, where *nnnn* is a number beginning at 0000. If errors occur in a file that contains extended attributes, CHKDSK recovers these lost clusters into files named EA*nnnn*.CHK.

If you answer no, CHKDSK deletes the lost clusters without further ado.

To determine whether a file consists of one single contiguous area of disk space or is divided up or *fragmented* into several separate pieces, specify a *filename* with CHKDSK. You can also include drive and path information if you wish. There is no harm in files becoming fragmented, although extreme fragmentation may slow down your hard disk performance.

• SWITCHES

The following switches are available for use on both FAT and HPFS disks.

/F   Tells CHKDSK to fix any errors found. This switch cannot be used when analyzing the hard disk that you use to start OS/2, nor can it be used on the disk that contains the CHKDSK program. If you have to run CHKDSK on your boot disk, you must first reboot your system using your original OS/2 Installation disk. When the logo panel appears, replace the Installation disk with disk 1, and press Enter to continue. When the Welcome to OS/2 screen appears, press the Escape key and insert the floppy disk that contains CHKDSK. Now run CHKDSK and specify drive C as the drive for analysis.

/V   Displays all files along with appropriate path information for the specified drive. This switch creates a very long file listing that is usually only of interest to system managers or to people concerned with software inventories.

The following switches are available only when using the HPFS.

/C   Recovers files only if the file system was in an inconsistent state when the computer was first started and files remain open. This might happen if the power failed during a disk operation before all the files could be closed.

/F   Specifies one of four recovery levels to be used:

/F:0 tells CHKDSK to analyze the file system and display the results, but not make any repairs.

/F:1 tells CHKDSK to resolve any inconsistent file-system structures.

/F:2 tells CHKDSK to resolve any inconsistent file-system structures and to scan the rest of the disk space in use to recover any recognizable directory or file elements not referenced by the file system.

/F:3 includes the /F:2 level recovery options, and also tells CHKDSK to scan the whole disk partition, looking for recognizable file-system elements.

If no recovery number is specified, F:2 is used as the default.

• EXAMPLES

To report on the degree of fragmentation of MYFILE.TXT, type

CHKDSK MYFILE.TXT

To make a listing of all the files on a disk, including appropriate path information, type

CHKDSK /V

Type the following to see a status report on drive C and fix any errors encountered:

CHKDSK C: /F

When using the HPFS, CHKDSK defaults to the /F level of repair. If you want to use the /F:3 level, type

CHKDSK /F:3

• **NOTES**   Remember that CHKDSK can only give accurate results when the disk being analyzed is not being used or actively written to by another session or application program.

In a DOS session, you cannot use CHKDSK on drives that have an ASSIGN, APPEND, JOIN, or SUBST command still in effect. Also, CHKDSK cannot be used on network drives.

There are also two limitations when using CHKDSK with the HPFS.

•   You cannot use a *filename* with CHKDSK when using the HPFS.

- If CHKDSK finds lost clusters under the HPFS, they are
  treated differently. When lost clusters are found and the
  /F switch was specified, CHKDSK creates a new directory
  called \FOUND.*nnn* below the root directory and places
  all directories, files, and extended attributes in this directory. The *nnn* directory extension represents a unique
  three-digit number so that each \FOUND directory name
  is unique. CHKDSK uses the FILE*nnnn*.CHK format
  for recovered files and the DIR*nnnn*.CHK format for
  recovered directories.

CLS

The CLS command clears the command interpreter screen or window except for the system prompt and the cursor. They are rewrit-
ten on the first line of the screen or window.

• SYNTAX AND DESCRIPTION

CLS

• Examples

To clear the screen or the window, type

CLS

CMD

OS/2

CMD starts a new OS/2 command processor. The command processor is the command-line interface that accepts and processes commands, loads and runs programs, and writes out error messages as necessary. To return to the original command processor, use the EXIT command.

• SYNTAX AND DESCRIPTION

CMD *drive:path /switches*

• SWITCHES

If you plan to use multiple switches with CMD, use the /Q or /S switches before you use the /K or /C switches.

/Q	Starts a new command processor in an echo off mode.
/S	Starts a new command processor and tells it to ignore any break characters (Ctrl+C).
/K "*string*"	Passes the contents of *string* to CMD.EXE, but does not return to the original command processor when the command contained in *string* is complete.
/C "*string*"	Passes the contents of *string* to CMD.EXE, and returns to the original command processor when the command contained in *string* is complete.

• EXAMPLES

To start a new command processor in echo off mode, type

CMD /Q

To start a new command processor, pass it a set of commands, and stay in the new environment, type

CMD /K "TYPE MYFILE.TXT"

• **NOTES** If you change any of the environment variables for the new command processor, these variables are only available to the new command processor; when you return to the original command processor, any changes are lost.

See also COMMAND, EXIT.

COMMAND

COMMAND starts a new DOS command processor. The command processor is the command-line interface that accepts and processes commands, loads and runs programs, and writes out error messages as necessary. To return to the original command processor, use the EXIT command.

• SYNTAX AND DESCRIPTION

COMMAND *drive: path /switches*

COMMAND used with no parameters starts a new command processor. The existing environment variables are duplicated for this new command processor, but if you change any of these settings, they are lost when you return to the original command processor. COMMAND expects to find the file containing the DOS command processor, COMMAND.COM, in a directory called C:\OS2\MSDOS. If the file is located elsewhere, use the appropriate path information.

• SWITCHES

/E:*nn*	Specifies the new size of the DOS environment. The range for a valid environment size extends from 160 bytes to 32,768 bytes, and is always rounded up to the nearest multiple of 16.
/P	Makes this new copy of the DOS command processor permanent until you restart OS/2 again.
/K *string*	Passes the contents of *string* to the new command processor, but does not return to the original command processor when the command contained in *string* is complete.
/C *string*	Passes the contents of *string* to the new command processor, and returns to the original command processor when the command contained in *string* is complete.

• EXAMPLES

To start a new permanent DOS command processor, type

COMMAND /P

If you want to enlarge the DOS environment space, type

COMMAND /E: 4096

To start a new command processor, run a command, and then return to the original command processor, type

COMMAND /C TYPE MYFILE.TXT

To repeat the previous example, but remain in the new DOS command processor, type

COMMAND /K TYPE MYFILE.TXT

• **NOTES**   If you use the SET command to change any of the environment variables for the new command processor, these variables are only available to the new command processor; when you return to the original command processor, any changes are lost.

This version of COMMAND does not include the MS-DOS 5 switch /MSG that stores all error messages in memory, so that floppy disk users do not have to keep a disk containing COMMAND.COM in drive A.

See also the CMD and EXIT entries in this section, and the SET entry in Part VI, "CONFIG.SYS Commands."

COMP

The COMP command compares the contents of two files, or two groups of files, to determine if the files are identical.

• **SYNTAX AND DESCRIPTION**

COMP *filename1 filename2*

filename1 and *filename2* specify the names of the files to be compared. You can use wildcard characters if you wish.

Type this command with no parameters, and you will be prompted to enter the file names you want to compare. If the files are not the same length, COMP informs you of this and asks if you want to continue with the comparison. If you answer yes, the comparison proceeds based on the length of the smaller of the two files. Results are displayed in hexadecimal on the screen, and an error is displayed for any information that does not match. After ten such mismatches, the comparison is automatically terminated, because it is obvious by this time that the two files are anything but identical.

• EXAMPLES

To have COMP ask you for the names of the files you want to compare, type

COMP

If you want to compare two files in your current directory, type

COMP MYFILE1.TXT MYFILE2.TXT

• **NOTES**   Unlike the MS-DOS 5 version of COMP, the OS/2 version does not accept any switches.

See also DISKCOMP.

COPY

The COPY command copies one or more files. You can also use COPY to rename, combine, append, or output files.

• SYNTAX AND DESCRIPTION

There are several different ways that you can use the COPY command, and the syntax varies slightly in each case. The most common use of the COPY command is to duplicate a file.

COPY *source filename* target filename /switches

The COPY command requires, as a minimum, a *source filename*, which can include wildcard characters, as well as drive and path information. You can also use a *target filename* which is usually another file name, and may contain a drive letter and path information. If the *target filename* contains only a directory name, the files are copied without changing their names.

The *source filename* and *target filename* cannot be the same file name in the same location on disk; in other words, COPY will not copy a file onto itself.

You can use a + sign to append one file to another, or to join several files together. The syntax now becomes

COPY *source filename* +*source filename+etc...***target filename**

You can also use wildcard characters when joining files in this way.

Finally, you can use COPY to change the date and time associated with a file, if you use the following syntax:

COPY *source filename +,,*

• SWITCHES

/A   Indicates that the file is an ASCII file. When used with the source file, the data in the file is copied up to but not including the first end-of-file character (Ctrl+Z) found in the file; the rest of the file is not copied. When used with the target file, this switch adds an end-of-file character as the final character in the file.

/B   Indicates that the file is a binary file. When used with the source file, the whole file is copied, based on information contained in the file's directory entries. When used with the target file, no end-of-file character is added as the last character in the file.

/F   Halts the COPY operation if you attempt to copy a file with OS/2 extended attributes onto a system that does not support these extended attributes.

/V   Makes the operating system check that all the sectors written on the destination disk are recorded correctly and without error. This switch slows down the COPY operation slightly, but you should use it when copying critical data.

• EXAMPLES

To copy a file called MYFILE.TXT from drive C to drive B, type

COPY C:\MYFILE.TXT B:

To copy OLDFILE.DOC from drive C to drive B and rename the file NEWFILE.DOC at the same time, type

COPY C:\OLDFILE.DOC B:\NEWFILE.DOC

If you want to join two ASCII files together and create a new file containing the result, use

COPY START.TXT + END.TXT /A WHOLE.TXT

To append or add one file to the end of another, type

COPY FIRST.TXT + SECOND.TXT

In this example, the file SECOND.TXT is added to the end of FIRST.TXT. Note that you do not have to specify a target file name.

Be careful that you understand what happens when you specify wildcard characters in file names with the COPY command. In this next example, let's assume that there are three files called ONE.BAK, TWO.BAK, and THREE.BAK, and three more files called ONE.DOC, TWO.DOC, and THREE.DOC. When you type

COPY *.BAK + *.DOC *.FIL

the results are as follows: The file ONE.FIL contains the combination of ONE.BAK and ONE.DOC, TWO.FIL contains TWO.BAK and TWO.DOC, and THREE.FIL contains THREE.BAK combined with THREE.DOC.

To change the time and date on all the files on the default drive to the current system time and date, type

COPY *.* /B +,,

If you want to use the COPY command to send a file to a peripheral device such as the printer, type

COPY README.TXT PRN

where PRN is the device name for the printer.

Finally, you can use the COPY command to copy characters from the standard input device, the console (which for our purposes we will consider to be the keyboard), and store them in an ASCII file. When you issue the COPY command, the screen waits for you to type characters from the keyboard.

COPY CON MYFILE

End each line of text with the Enter key, and when you have entered all the information, press function key F6 (or Ctrl+Z) to place an end-of-file character at the end of the file, followed by the Enter key.

• **NOTES**   When using the COPY command with a device such as a printer, make sure that the printer is online and ready to receive the information.

See also DISKCOPY, MOVE, REN, VERIFY, XCOPY.

CREATEDD

The CREATEDD command creates a Dump disk for use with the Stand-Alone Dump procedure that creates an image of all the physical memory available on your system. This is only done as a troubleshooting aid when a problem is especially difficult to reproduce, and is only done at the request of a service technician or a technical support person.

DATE

The DATE command displays or resets the system clock. Special circuitry inside your computer automatically keeps track of the date, even when the computer is turned off, so it is not usually necessary to reset the date, even at the end of the month or the end of the year.

• SYNTAX AND DESCRIPTION

DATE *mm-dd-yy*

The month is specified by *mm*, and must be a number between 1 and 12. The day is specified by *dd*, and must be between 1 and 31. Years, *yy*, are entered using the numbers from 00 to 99, where 00 to 79 represent the years from 2000 to 2079.

You can use a slash (/), a period (.), or a dash (-) as the separating character between entries.

• EXAMPLES

To set the system clock to January 1, 1994, type

DATE 01-01-94

If you want to see the current system date, type

DATE

then either type in a new date or press the Enter key to return to the operating system without changing the date.

• NOTES   See also TIME.

DDINSTAL

The DDINSTAL command lets you install new device drivers after the operating system has been installed.

• SYNTAX AND DESCRIPTION

DDINSTAL

Enter this command with no parameters to start a step-by-step procedure for installing new device drivers that come with a Device Support Disk. This disk contains a Device Driver Profile (DDP) file that controls the driver installation process. DDINSTAL uses information found in this file to copy the correct statements into your CONFIG.SYS file, and to copy all of the support files into the right directories on your hard disk. After DDINSTAL has loaded the device drivers, press Ctrl, Alt, and Delete to restart your system.

• EXAMPLES

When you type

DDINSTAL

OS/2 guides you through a short procedure for installing new device drivers.

• NOTES   See also the DEVICE command in Part VI, "CONFIG.SYS Commands."

DEBUG

The DEBUG command allows you to display, test, and debug executable files.

• SYNTAX AND DESCRIPTION

DEBUG *drive: path filename*

drive: path filename specifies the name of the executable file that you want to debug.

When you use the DEBUG command, you enter the DOS debug environment and the command prompt changes to a dash. Type a question mark to see a list of all the commands available in the debug environment, as follows:

?	Lists all the commands available in DEBUG.
A	Assembles 8086/8087/8088 assembly-language mnemonics.
C	Compares two areas of memory.
D	Displays the contents of an area of memory as hexadecimal and ASCII values.
E	Enters data into memory starting at a specific address.
F	Fills an area of memory with a specific value.
G	Runs the executable file that is in memory.
H	Performs hexadecimal arithmetic on two numbers.
I	Inputs and displays a one-byte value from a port at the specified address.
L	Loads a program file or a specified number of disk sectors from a program file into memory.

M   Moves the contents of an area of memory.

N   Specifies a file for use with the L or W commands.

O   Sends a one-byte value to the specified output port.

P   Executes a program, subroutine, loop, or interrupt.

Q   Quits DEBUG.

R   Displays or changes the contents of registers.

S   Searches an area of memory for a specific pattern of
        byte values.

T   Enters trace mode and steps though a specified
        number of instructions one at a time, displaying the
        contents of all registers.

U   Unassembles bytes and displays the appropriate
        source statements.

W   Writes the current file or a specified number of disk
        sectors from memory to disk.

XA   Allocates the specified number of 16K pages into
        expanded memory.

XD   Deallocates expanded memory.

XM   Maps expanded memory pages.

XS   Displays the status of expanded memory.

• EXAMPLES

To access DEBUG, type

DEBUG

at the DOS command prompt.

• NOTES   Debugging a program is not an everyday task for most
users; it is a job best left to programmers. Also, most modern computer
language compilers have much more capable and advanced debugging
aids available to them than the DEBUG command.

DEL

The DEL command erases one or more files, and is used inter-changeably with the ERASE command.

• SYNTAX AND DESCRIPTION

DEL *drive:\path**filename** /switches*

The *drive:\path\filename* specifies the name of the file you want to delete, and may contain wildcard characters if you want to erase a group of files all at the same time.

If you use the wildcard specification *.* with the DEL command, it means that you want to delete all the files in the current directory. Because this is a potentially dangerous command, the operating system responds with the prompt

Are you sure (Y/N)?

Type a Y (yes) if you are sure you want to proceed, or type N (no) to cancel the command. Using a directory name in a DEL command is the same as specifying all the files in that directory. If you want to erase a directory once it is empty, you must use the RD command.

The DEL command cannot erase files that have the read-only or hidden attribute set.

• SWITCHES

/N   Tells the DEL command not to display the *Are you sure (Y/N)?* message when you are deleting the entire contents of a directory. Most people find this message is a useful reminder that they are about to perform a potentially dangerous delete operation; others find it annoying. If you are in this latter category, you can turn the message off.

/P   Tells the DEL command to ask you if you want to delete each file individually when you issue a DEL *.* command.

• EXAMPLES

To delete a single file called MONDAY from the current directory, type

DEL MONDAY

To delete all the files in the current directory with the file-name extension .BAK, use

DEL *.BAK

If you want to erase all the files in the current directory, type

DEL *.*

The operating system responds with the message *Are you sure (Y/N)?*. Type a Y to continue the delete operation and erase all the files in the directory; type N to cancel the command.

You can also delete all the files in a directory if you use the directory name in a DEL command. If the current directory contains a subdirectory called \DAILY, you can delete all the files in this directory if you type

DEL DAILY

You will also see the *Are you sure (Y/N)?* message here too, unless you use the /N switch, as follows:

DEL DAILY /N

To review each file name in a directory before deciding if you want
to delete it, use

DEL *.* /P

This switch is very useful if you want to delete some of the files
from a directory but keep others, particularly when the files do not
share common file-name extensions and so wildcards are of little
use in differentiating between groups of files.

• **NOTES**   The OS/2 DEL /N switch is not available in MS-DOS 5.

You may be able to recover files that you erase by accident if you
use the UNDELETE command immediately upon discovering the
mistake. Do not use the computer for any other operation until you
have recovered any accidentally deleted files; there is always the
chance that you might overwrite the deleted files before you can
recover them. See the entry for UNDELETE later in this section for
more information.

See also RD, UNDELETE.

DETACH

The DETACH command starts an OS/2 program and immediately
detaches it from its command processor and runs the program in
the background. The command processor continues to run in the
foreground.

• **SYNTAX AND DESCRIPTION**

DETACH *command*

The *command* parameter can be any OS/2 program or command
that does not need input from the keyboard or mouse and does not

output anything to the screen. Any program started with DETACH must be able to operate without the services of the command processor.

• EXAMPLES

To run a batch program called MYFILE.CMD in the background, while the OS/2 command processor continues to run in the foreground, type

DETACH MYFILE.CMD

The DIR command lists the contents of a directory, along with additional disk file storage information.

• SYNTAX AND DESCRIPTION

DIR *drive:\path\filename /switches*

If you use DIR with no parameters, the command displays the contents of the current directory, both files and subdirectories. You can also use wildcard characters with DIR to display only those files that match the wildcard specification.

The DIR command usually lists the following information:

- Disk volume label
- Disk volume serial number
- Directory name
- File names and extensions
- Subdirectory names

- File sizes in bytes
- Date and time of file creation or last modification
- Total number of files in the directory
- Amount of disk space used, in bytes
- Amount of disk space remaining, in bytes

The DIR command does not show files that have the hidden or system attributes set, even if they are present in the directory, unless you use a special switch.

• SWITCHES

/W   Selects a wide-display format capable of listing five columns of file names on an 80-character display.

/F   Displays just the drive letter, directory name, and file name for each entry. This is known as the *fully qualified file* name. The special directory entries . and .. are not shown

/A   Displays only those files and directories that possess the attributes you specify. You can use any combination of these attributes you like but do not separate them with spaces. You can use the following:

A = Files ready to backup or archive

-A = Files unchanged since the last backup

D = Directories, but not files

-D = Files, but not directories

H = Hidden files

-H = Files that are not hidden

R = Read-only files

-R = Files that are not read-only

S = System files

-S = Files that are not system files

/B   Removes the heading information and file summary from the directory listing.

/L   Displays information in lowercase.

/N   Displays files created using the FAT file system in the format used for the HPFS directory listings. This includes

        • The date that the file was created or modified

        • The time that the file was created or modified

        • The size of the file in bytes, or <DIR> if the entry is a directory

        • The size of the file's extended attributes, in bytes

        • The file name

     When you use the HPFS, the extended attribute information is always shown in a directory listing, regardless of whether you use the /N switch.

/O   Displays the files and directories in the sort order you specify, from the following options:

     D = Date and time, earliest first

     -D = Date and time, latest first

     E = Alphabetical order of file-name extension

     -E = Reverse alphabetical order of file-name extension

     G = Directories listed first, before files

     -G = Files listed first, before directories

     N = Alphabetical order of file name

     -N = Reverse alphabetical order of file name

     S = Size, smallest first

     -S = Size, largest first

/P   Displays one screenful of entries and then pauses. To see the next screen, press any key.

/R   Displays long file names, even when you use the FAT
      file system. For example, you will see the name OS/2
      2.0 Desktop opposite the OS!2_2.0_D directory entry.

/S   Lists all occurrences of the specified file in the current
      directory, and in all subdirectories of the current
      directory.

• EXAMPLES

To display the contents of the current directory, type

DIR

If you want to see the listing in the five-column format, type

DIR / W

To list all the files in the current directory with the file name extension .BAK, use

DIR *.BAK

and if there are too many of these files to fit on a single screen, use
the /P switch to display the information one screen at a time:

DIR *.BAK /P

If you want to see the entries listed in HPFS format, type

DIR /N

To see a listing of all the executable files in all the directories and
subdirectories on the current disk, change to the root directory,
and type

DIR *.EXE /S

and to sort these entries into alphabetical order by file name, use

DIR *.EXE /S /ON

• NOTES   The OS/2 DIR switches /F, /N, and /R have no corresponding equivalent in MS-DOS 5.

If you use the /P or /W switches in a DOS window, you may not be able to see all the entries. Maximize the window before using the command or open a DOS session in full-screen mode.

See also CD, MD, RD, TREE.

DISKCOMP

The DISKCOMP command compares the contents of two disks. The disks must be of the same type, with the same size and density.

• SYNTAX AND DESCRIPTION

DISKCOMP *source drive target drive*

The parameters *source drive* and *target drive* specify the drives that contain the disks to be compared. DISKCOMP compares the contents of two floppy disks, track by track, to determine if they are identical. Both disks must be of the same size and density; you cannot use DISKCOMP to compare 3½" and 5¼" disks. However, you can compare two different disks using the same drive, and the DISKCOMP command prompts you when it is time to swap disks.

• EXAMPLES

To compare the contents of a 3½" floppy disk in drive A, with the contents of another 3½" floppy disk in drive B, type

DISKCOMP A: B:

If you want to compare two 5¼" disks using drive A, your only 5¼" drive, type

DISKCOMP A: A:

and the DISKCOMP command will guide you through the comparison, prompting you to swap the disks when necessary.

• **NOTES**   DISKCOMP does not work in a DOS session when ASSIGN, JOIN, or SUBST commands are in effect. Also, DISKCOMP does not work on network drives.

Unlike the MS-DOS 5 version of DISKCOMP, the OS/2 version does not accept any switches.

See also DISKCOPY.

DISKCOPY

The DISKCOPY command copies the contents of one floppy disk onto another floppy disk of identical size and density. The target floppy disk will be formatted if necessary.

• SYNTAX AND DESCRIPTION

DISKCOPY *source drive target drive*

The parameters *source drive* and *target drive* specify the drives that contain the floppy disks you want to copy to and from.

DISKCOPY makes an exact duplicate of the source disk to the extent that if there are data errors on the source disk, they will be faithfully reproduced on the target disk. Also, if the files on the source disk are badly fragmented, so will be the files on the target disk at the end of the DISKCOPY operation. If it is important to reduce file fragmentation, use the XCOPY command to copy the contents of the source disk. See the XCOPY entry later in this section for more information.

You should use the DISKCOPY command when you make a backup copy of your original program disks, because these disks must be *exact* copies of the originals, including any hidden or system files and volume labels. The COPY and XCOPY commands will not copy these important elements.

You cannot use DISKCOPY to copy the contents of hard disks, RAM disks, or different kinds or sizes of floppy disk. Use the COPY or XCOPY commands instead.

You can use DISKCOPY to duplicate a disk using just one floppy disk drive, however. DISKCOPY prompts you when it is time to change the source and target disks over. It is a good idea to write-protect the source floppy disk, because it can be easy to confuse source and target disks if you are interrupted during the DISK-COPY process.

If the target disk is an unformatted blank disk, DISKCOPY will format the disk so that it matches the source disk.

• EXAMPLES

To make an exact copy of a 3½" disk in drive A onto another 3½" disk in drive B, type

DISKCOPY A: B:

If you want to copy a disk using just one drive, drive A, type

DISKCOPY A: A:

and the DISKCOPY command will prompt you when it is time to swap the disks over.

• NOTES
Because OS/2 is a multitasking operating system, it is possible that another system command or application program might attempt to write on one of the floppy disks used in a DISK-COPY operation. OS/2 prevents this from happening by locking the disks; once the DISKCOPY operation is complete, the floppy disks are unlocked and available for use once more.

The DISKCOPY command does not work on drives affected by AS-SIGN, JOIN, or SUBST commands.

Unlike the MS-DOS 5 version of DISKCOPY, the OS/2 version does not accept any switches.

See also COPY, DISKCOMP, XCOPY.

DOSKEY

The DOSKEY command installs the DOSKEY program that lets you recall and edit the DOS command line, as well as create and run small command-line macros.

• SYNTAX AND DESCRIPTION

DOSKEY */switches macroname=text*

The DOSKEY program is a small terminate-and-stay resident program that gives you more flexibility to edit the DOS command line and work with macros. If you invoke DOSKEY with no parameters, the program loads using its default settings. DOSKEY saves everything you type at the command line, legal commands as well as mistakes.

DOSKEY uses the following keys to recall a command:

↑	Recalls the previous DOS command.
↓	Recalls the next DOS command in the queue.
PgUp	Recalls the oldest DOS command in this session.
PgDn	Recalls the most recent DOS command in this session.

To edit the command line, use these DOSKEY editing keys:

←	Moves the cursor one character to the left.
→	Moves the cursor one character to the right.
Ctrl+←	Moves the cursor one word to the left.
Ctrl+→	Moves the cursor one word to the right.
Home	Moves the cursor to the beginning of the line.
End	Moves the cursor to the end of the line.
Esc	Clears the command from the screen.
F1	Copies one character from the memory buffer to the command line.
F2	Searches forward through the memory buffer up to the next key you type after pressing F2.
F3	Copies the contents of the memory buffer to the command line.
F4	Deletes characters from the memory buffer, up to the first character typed after pressing F4.
F5	Copies the current command line into the memory buffer, clearing the command line in the process.
F6	Adds an end-of-file character (Ctrl+Z) to the end of the current command line.
F7	Displays all the commands stored in the memory buffer, along with their associated sequence numbers.
Alt+F7	Deletes all the commands stored in the memory buffer.
F8	Searches memory for a command. Type F8, then type the beginning of the command, then type F8 again.
F9	Asks for a sequence number and displays the command associated with that number.
Alt+F10	Deletes all the macro definitions.

DOSKEY 117

When creating a macro, the following commands are available:

$b	Sends macro output to a command. This is equivalent to the pipe (ǀ) redirection symbol.
$g	Redirects output to a device rather than sending the output to the screen. This is equivalent to the normal redirection symbol (>).
gg	Adds output to the end of a file rather than overwriting the file. Equivalent to the normal symbols for appending redirected output (>>).
$l	Redirects input, equivalent to (<<).
$t	A separating character used to separate commands in a macro.
$$	Specifies the dollar sign should you ever wish to use one in a macro.
$1 through $9	Placeholder symbols used to allow you to specify different information on the command line each time you run the macro. The $1 character in a DOSKEY macro is similar in function to the %1 character in a batch program.
$*	Holds all the command-line information you specify when you run your macro. Everything you type on the command line after the macro name is substituted for the $* in the macro.

None of these macro-creating commands are case-sensitive; you can use $g or $G as you wish.

• SWITCHES

/REINSTALL	Installs a new copy of the DOSKEY program, even if a copy is currently installed, and empties the memory buffer.

/BUFSIZE=*nnn*	Specifies the size of the memory buffer. The default size of *nnn* is 512 bytes, the minimum size is 256 bytes.
/H	Displays a list of the commands stored in memory.
/M ·	Displays a list of all the DOSKEY macros.
/OVERSTRIKE	Specifies that any new text you type will replace existing text. /OVERSTRIKE is the default setting. Cannot be used with /INSERT.
/INSERT	Specifies that any new text you type will be inserted into the existing text. Cannot be used with /OVERSTRIKE.
macroname=text	Creates a macro that processes one or more DOS commands. *macroname* specifies the name of the macro, while *text* represents the commands you want to use in the macro.

• EXAMPLES

To load DOSKEY for the first time, type

DOSKEY

You can now use any of the command editing commands as described above; use the ↑ key to recall the previous command, or PgUp to see the first command of this DOSKEY session.

If you want to create a macro called WP that will start your copy of WordPerfect from the /WP51 directory, type

DOSKEY WP = CD\WP51$TWP.EXE

To run the WP macro, type

WP

and WordPerfect will start running.

• **NOTES**   Because all DOSKEY macros are stored in memory rather than on disk, they are lost when you turn your computer off. Also, you cannot invoke a macro from inside a batch program.

The OS/2 equivalent of DOSKEY is the KEYS command.

See also KEYS.

EAUTIL

The EAUTIL command lets you detach and save extended attributes from a file so that the file can be used by an application that does not recognize these attributes. When the application is finished, you can use EAUTIL to reattach the extended attributes.

• SYNTAX AND DESCRIPTION

EAUTIL *datafile* *holdfile* */switches*

Not all application programs running under OS/2 understand how to use a file's extended attributes, so EAUTIL offers a method of splitting these attributes off from the file and saving them in a secure place. You can then use EAUTIL to rejoin them back on to the original file when the application program is finished. This prevents the extended attributes from being erased or lost by accident. You can use the DIR command with the /R switch to see if your files include extended attributes.

The *datafile* parameter specifies the file whose extended attributes will be split off and stored in the file specified by the *holdfile* parameter. If no *holdfile* is specified, EAUTIL creates a hold file with the same name as the data file and places it in a new subdirectory of the current directory called EAS.

• SWITCHES

/S   Separates extended attributes from a file and stores them in a hold file.

/R   Replaces the extended attributes in the hold file with those from the data file.

/J   Reconnects the extended attributes in the hold file to the data file.

/O   Overwrites or deletes the extended attributes in the data file with the extended attributes from the hold file.

/M   Merges the extended attributes from the hold file with those in the data file.

/P   Copies extended attributes to or from a data file or a hold file without deleting the original copy of the extended attributes.

• EXAMPLES

If you want to split the extended attributes from MYFILE.TXT, and save them in the default hold file called MYFILE.TXT in the new subdirectory created by EAUTIL called EAS, type

EAUTIL MYFILE.TXT /S

To reattach the extended attributes to MYFILE.TXT, type

EAUTIL MYFILE.TXT EAS\MYFILE.TXT /J

• NOTES   See also IFS.

ERASE

See DEL.

EXIT

The EXIT command ends or closes the current command processor and returns to the previous command processor or to the desktop if no previous session exists.

• SYNTAX AND DESCRIPTION

EXIT

• EXAMPLES

If you want to leave the current OS/2 or DOS session, type

EXIT

• **NOTES**   If you are running an application program, you must close the program before invoking EXIT.

See also CMD, COMMAND.

FDISK

The FDISK command lets you create or delete a primary hard disk partition or a logical drive in an extended hard disk partition. This is an advanced command and must be used with care.

• SYNTAX AND DESCRIPTION

FDISK /switches /options

If you type FDISK with no switches, the menu-driven portion of the program opens to guide you through hard disk partition configuration. This mode of operation is much easier to use if you are unfamiliar with FDISK, but you can also work with FDISK directly from the command line, specifying switches and switch options as needed.

Remember that the switch must appear in the command line before the appropriate limiting option.

All hard disks are divided up into partitions. A partition can be defined as that part of a disk that belongs to a particular operating system, and it may in fact occupy the whole disk. Although a hard disk can be divided into several primary partitions and/or one extended partition, the first hard disk on a system must have a primary partition. An extended partition can be further subdivided into smaller logical drives for convenience sake.

• SWITCHES

/QUERY

Displays a list of all the partitions on the hard disk.

/CREATE:*name*

Creates a primary partition or logical drive in an extended partition with the optional *name*. Specify the type of partition to create using the /VTYPE:*n* option described below.

/DELETE

Deletes a logical drive or partition.

/SETNAME:*name*

Establishes a *name* for primary partitions or logical drives, and makes them bootable from the Boot Manager; if *name* is not specified, then the partition will not be bootable.

/SETACCESS	Makes a primary DOS partition accessible. Once this is done, all other primary DOS partitions on the same drive become inaccessible.
/STARTABLE	Specifies a partition as startable.
/FILE:*filename*	Processes FDISK commands contained in the response file called *filename*.

The following options are used to limit the scope of the switches described above:

/switch/NAME:*name*	Specifies the name of a partition. This option can be used with all FDISK switches except /FILE and /SETACCESS.
/switch/DISK:*n*	Specifies the number of the hard disk. This option can be used with all FDISK switches except /FILE.
/switch/FSTYPE:*x*	Specifies the file system type of the partition. Type *x* can represent DOS, FAT, IFS, FREE, or other. This option cannot be used with the /FILE or /SETACCESS switches.
/switch/START:*m*	Specifies the partition starting location, where *m* can be *t* for the top of the partition, or *b* for the bottom. /START cannot be used with /FILE.
/switch/SIZE:*m*	Specifies the size of the partition in MB. This option cannot be use with the /FILE switch.
/switch/VTYPE:*n*	Specifies the type of the partition, where *n* can be

0 = unusable space

1 = primary partition

	2 = logical drive
	3 = display free space
	/VTYPE can be used with all FDISK switches except /FILE, /SETACCESS, or /STARTABLE
/switch/BOOTABLE:*s*	Indicates the bootable status of the partition; *s* is 0 for a nonbootable partition, or 1 for a bootable partition. The /BOOTABLE option can be used with all FDISK switches except /FILE.
/BOOTMGR	This option indicates that the switch is intended for the Boot Manager partition.

• EXAMPLES

To see a display of the partitions on your system, type

FDISK /QUERY

If you want to create a new logical drive in an extended partition on drive 1 with the name MYDRIVE, type

FDISK /CREATE:MYDRIVE / VTYPE:2 /DISK:1

To delete the logical drive called MYDRIVE, use the following:

FDISK /DELETE /NAME:MYDRIVE

• NOTES   FDISK cannot be run in an OS/2 DOS session, and cannot
work with drives with current ASSIGN, JOIN, or SUBST commands.

Careless use of the FDISK command can permanently destroy hard disk data. Use the command with caution. The best insurance is a complete, up-to-date backup of all your files.

The MS-DOS 5 version of FDISK does not accept switches.

See also FDISKPM, SETBOOT.

FDISKPM

The FDISKPM command lets you create or delete a primary hard disk partition or a logical drive in an extended hard disk partition. This is an advanced command and must be used with care.

• SYNTAX AND DESCRIPTION

FDISKPM

The FDISKPM command opens an OS/2 mouse-and-window-based program that helps you manage the hard disk partitioning process using selections from the Options menu. You can use selections from this menu to

- Install the Boot Manager partition.

- Create or delete a primary partition or a logical drive.

- Add or change a partition name.

- Set startup values such as the default partition.

- Remove a partition from the Boot Manager menu.

- Set a primary partition as installable.

- Specify a primary partition to be a startable partition.

• EXAMPLES

To run FDISKPM, type the following at the OS/2 command prompt:

FDISKPM

• NOTES   FDISKPM cannot be run in an OS/2 DOS session.

See also FDISK, SETBOOT.

FIND

 OS/2   DOS

The FIND command searches a file or files for a specified text string.

• SYNTAX AND DESCRIPTION

FIND /switches **"string"** drive\path**filename**

The FIND command searches through the file or files that you specify looking for the characters contained in the *"string"*. These search characters must be contained within quotes and must be in the same case (uppercase or lowercase) as the text in the file. For example, the string "OS/2" is not the same as the string "os/2". If the text you are looking for is already contained within quotes inside the file, then you must use two sets of quotes with the FIND command. See the Examples section that follows for more information.

• SWITCHES

In the FIND command, remember to place the switches you want to use before the search string. In most OS/2 commands, the switches are placed at the end of the command-line entry.

/C   Counts the lines that contain the search string. If you use /C in combination with /V, FIND counts the lines that do not contain the search string.

/I   Tells FIND to ignore case differences when looking for the search string. When you use the /I switch, OS/2 and os/2 *are* considered to be equivalent.

/N   Adds a line number before the display of each match. This switch cannot be used with /C.

/V   Displays all the lines that do not contain the search string.

• EXAMPLES

To count the number of times that the word *Elvis* appears in the file ROCKSTAR, type

FIND /C "Elvis" ROCKSTAR

To display the line number in the file where the text *Elvis* appears, use

FIND /N "Elvis" ROCKSTAR

To locate the text contained in quotes *"Go west, young man"* in the file BOOK.TXT, use the following FIND command:

FIND ""Go west, young man"" BOOK.TXT

• **NOTES**   When you use the FIND command, you must explicitly state all the file names you want to search; you cannot use the wildcard characters * or ? in file names.

FORMAT

The FORMAT command prepares the disk in the specified drive for use by the operating system, and checks the disk for defects. The FORMAT command also creates the system area on the disk that contains the root directory and the file allocation tables.

• SYNTAX AND DESCRIPTION

FORMAT *drive* /*switches*

The FORMAT command performs several different tasks in preparing a disk for use:

- It creates a set of sectors and tracks that the operating system can use when storing data.

- It checks the disk media for physical defects, and marks defective areas so that they will not be used.

- It creates the system area on the disk that includes the root directory and file allocation tables.

- It assigns a volume serial number to a newly formatted disk.

- It lets you add a volume label to describe the contents of the disk.

If you format a floppy or hard disk that already contains information, all of the original information will be obliterated and lost.

If you format a drive for use with the HPFS, the FORMAT command checks the IFS statement in your CONFIG.SYS file to see if there is an /AUTOCHECK parameter for the drive. If the drive is listed, FORMAT does not update the IFS statement; if not, FORMAT adds the drive letter.

Make sure that you use the FDISK or FDISKPM commands to establish an OS/2 partition on a hard disk before you format it. If no DOS or OS/2 partition exists, FORMAT will not recognize the disk as being an OS/2 disk, and will not format the disk but will skip over it to the next disk.

● SWITCHES

/ONCE   Tells the FORMAT command that you only intend to format one disk, and so when FORMAT has finished, it does not ask if you want to format another disk.

/4   Formats a 360K floppy disk in a 1.2MB disk drive. Not all 360K disk drives will be able to read this disk, so use this switch with caution.

/F:*nnn*   Specifies the capacity to which the disk will be
                  formatted; FORMAT creates the appropriate
                  number of tracks and sectors. The FORMAT
                  command is very flexible, and you can specify
                  the capacity for the disk in a variety of different
                  ways, as follows:

        360K 5.25" disk = 360, 360K, 360KB

        720K 3.5" disk = 720, 720K, 720KB

        1.2MB 5.25" disk = 1200, 1200K, 1200KB, 1.2,
1.2M, 1.2MB

        1.44MB 3.5" disk = 1440, 1440K, 1440KB, 1.44,
1.44M, 1.44MB

        2.88MB 3.5" disk = 2880, 2880K, 2880KB, 2.88,
2.88M, 2.88MB

/FS:*name*   Specifies that the FORMAT command should
                  execute another file system's format program
                  name.

/L   Specifies the long format procedure for use
                  with IBM's read/write optical disk. It takes
                  about 20 minutes. This switch also installs a file
                  system on the optical disk.

/N:*sectors*   Formats a floppy disk to the specified number
                  of sectors.

/T:*nnn*   Formats a floppy disk to the specified number of
                  tracks. If /T is not specified, the default value of
                  80 tracks is used.

/V:*label*   Specifies a volume label for the disk.

Use the following values for /N (sectors) and /T (tracks) according
to the floppy disk size:

360K 5.25"	/T:40	/N:9
720K 3.5"	/T:80	/N:9
1.2MB 5.25"	/T:80	/N15

| 1.44MB 3.5" | /T:80 /N:18 |
| 2.88MB 3.5" | /T:80 /N:36 |

• EXAMPLES

To format one 3.5" high-density floppy disk in drive B, type

FORMAT B: /ONCE

If you want to format a 720K 3.5" disk in a 1.44MB floppy disk drive in drive A, use the following:

FORMAT A: /T:80 /N:9

Alternatively, you could use

FORMAT A: /F:720

instead.

To add the text *Budgets* as a volume label to a disk formatted in drive B, type

FORMAT B: /V:Budgets

To format a partition on drive D with the HPFS, type the following:

FORMAT D: /FS:HPSF

To format the partition as a FAT partition, use

FORMAT D: /FS:FAT

• NOTES   Never try to format a floppy disk to an incorrect capacity; you will lose data.

The FORMAT command does not work on network drives or on drives with ASSIGN, JOIN, or SUBST commands in effect.

The OS/2 FORMAT command does not have switches that correspond to the MS-DOS 5 /S switch to create a bootable disk, or to the /Q switch that performs a quick format without destroying data.

See also FDISK, FDISKPM, IFS.

FSACCESS

 DOS

The FSACCESS command accesses a drive using the OS/2 file system during a specific DOS session.

• SYNTAX AND DESCRIPTION

For FSACCESS to work, the device driver FSFILTER must be installed as the first DEVICE = statement in your CONFIG.SYS file. See Part VI for more information.

Once FSFILTER is installed, there are three main ways you can use FSACCESS, as follows:

FSACCESS *DOSdriveletter*

where *DOSdriveletter* specifies a particular local drive letter. The following colon is optional.

FSACCESS *DOSdriveletter - DOSdriveletter*

The minus sign and second drive letter indicates an inclusive range of drive letters.

FSACCESS *DOSdriveletter = OS/2driveletter*

In this case the equals sign maps a local DOS drive letter to an OS/2 drive letter. Again the following colon is optional.

In most circumstances, your DOS drive letters are assigned the same drive letters for OS/2 drives. To check the current mappings, use the FSACCESS command with no parameters. To change the mapping, use the FSACCESS command and the appropriate drive letter. To indicate that a drive should not be mapped, use an exclamation point before the drive letter.

• EXAMPLES

To check the drive mappings in existence now, type

FSACCESS

To give a DOS drive access to the OS/2 file system, type

FSACCESS J:

All references to drive J will now be sent to the OS/2 file system. Use the minus sign to include a range of drives:

FSACCESS J: - M:

You can use an equals sign to map a DOS drive to a different OS/2 drive, if you type

FSACCESS C: = E:

Use an exclamation point to tell OS/2 not to allow a drive access to the OS/2 file system, as follows:

FSACCESS !J:

To remove a mapping, use

FSACCESS "J:

• NOTES   You cannot remap the current drive.

See also FSFILTER.

GRAFTABL

The GRAFTABL command allows a DOS session to display the characters in the extended ASCII character set (numbers 128 through 255). The command has no effect in OS/2 sessions.

• SYNTAX AND DESCRIPTION

GRAFTABL *nnn /switches*

In the GRAFTABL command, *nnn* specifies a three-digit number to indicate the code page to use, from the following:

437   United States

850   Multilingual

860   Portuguese

863   French Canadian

865   Nordic

• SWITCHES

?   Displays a short summary of code-page options as well as the number of the graphics code page in use.

/STA   Displays the number of the graphics code page currently in use.

• EXAMPLES

To display the number of the graphic code page in use, type

GRAFTABL /STA

To change to the US GRAFTABL, type

GRAFTABL 437

• NOTES   See also CHCP, MODE.

HELP

The HELP command provides several ways to get help information when you are at the DOS or OS/2 command prompts.

• SYNTAX AND DESCRIPTION

HELP *switches*

Some DOS commands display a short help screen if you add the /? switch at the command prompt.

If you type HELP without switches at the OS/2 or DOS prompts, you will see a list of commands you can use to switch between sessions and get help on different topics.

• SWITCHES

ON	Turns on the help line at the top of the screen.
OFF	Turns off the help line at the top of the screen.
message number	Requests help on a specific system error number. You do not have to type the message prefix or the leading zeros.
book	Identifies the book or .INF file you want to search for information. If you do not specify a name, HELP searches the *OS/2 Command Reference* by default.
topic	Identifies the topic you want information on.

• EXAMPLES

To turn the help line on, type

HELP ON

To turn it off again, type

HELP OFF

This command only refers to the help line; all other help features will continue to work normally.

A very common error in OS/2 is *SYS0002: The system cannot find the file specified*. To see a longer explanation of what this message means, type

HELP 2

You do not have to type all the characters that precede the actual message number.

To see information from the *OS/2 Command Reference* on the FDISKPM command, type the following from the OS/2 command prompt:

HELP CMDREF FDISKPM

The desktop returns to the screen and opens the *OS/2 Command Reference* on the screen.

• NOTES   See also VIEW.

JOIN

DOS

The JOIN command connects the directory structure on a disk drive to a specific directory on a different drive. You can only JOIN a drive at the root directory.

• SYNTAX AND DESCRIPTION

JOIN *drive1: drive2:\path /switches*

The JOIN command allows programs that were written to access a particular drive to access a directory instead.

drive1 represents the drive that you want to connect to a directory on a different drive, while *drive2:\path* represents an empty directory in the root of the second drive; if this directory does not exist, OS/2 creates it for you.

While a drive is joined, it is no longer recognized by the operating system, and cannot be accessed directly; if you try, you will see an error message.

To see a list of the currently joined drives on your system, use JOIN with no parameters.

• SWITCHES

/D   Cancels a JOIN.

• EXAMPLES

To join drive B to the path C:\DRIVEB, and access drive B using the \DRIVEB subdirectory, type

JOIN B: C:\DRIVEB

To cancel the join, use

JOIN /D

• **NOTES**   You cannot JOIN the current drive, and you cannot use the following commands on joined drives: ASSIGN, BACKUP, CHKDSK, DISKCOMP, DISKCOPY, FORMAT, LABEL, RECOVER, RESTORE.

KEYB

OS/2

The KEYB command chooses a keyboard layout that replaces the current keyboard layout for all OS/2 and DOS full-screen sessions and all OS/2 window sessions.

• SYNTAX AND DESCRIPTION

KEYB *layout subcountry*

The KEYB command is a quick way to change keyboard layout if you include a DEVINFO statement in your CONFIG.SYS file. See Part VI for more information about CONFIG.SYS and the DEVINFO command.

Type KEYB with no parameters to see the current settings for KEYB as well as information on the current code page.

If you want to change your keyboard layout, specify *layout* as one of the two-letter codes from the following list.

AR   Arabic

BE   Belgium

CF   Canada (French)

CS	Czechoslovakia
DK	Denmark
SU	Finland
FR	France
GR	Germany
HE	Hebrew
HU	Hungary
IS	Iceland
IT	Italy
LA	Latin America
NL	Netherlands
NO	Norway
PL	Poland
PO	Portugal
SP	Spain
SV	Sweden
SF	Switzerland (French)
SG	Switzerland (German)
TR	Turkey
UK	United Kingdom
US	United States
YU	Yugoslavia

Add a *subcountry* code for countries that have more than one layout.

243, 245	Czechoslovakia
189, 120	France
141, 142	Italy
166, 168	United Kingdom

• EXAMPLES

To change to the UK keyboard, type

KEYB UK

• NOTES   Run this command from a full-screen OS/2 session; do not use it from an OS/2 window session, because unexpected results may occur.

It is very easy to arrive at the point where the keyboard layout and code page in memory are out of synchronization. To avoid this, make sure that the KEYB command and the CODEPAGE command in CONFIG.SYS both specify the same country.

The OS/2 version of KEYB does not support any of the MS-DOS 5 switches, such as /E for the extended keyboard.

See also CHCP in this section and also the CODEPAGE, COUNTRY, and DEVINFO entries in Part VI, "CONFIG.SYS Commands."

KEYS

The KEYS command lets you retrieve and edit commands previously issued from the OS/2 command prompt.

• SYNTAX AND DESCRIPTION

KEYS *switches*

Use the command with no parameters to see the current status of the KEYS command.

When KEYS is turned on you can use the following editing commands:

Esc	Clears the command line and returns the cursor to the command prompt.
Home	Moves the cursor to the beginning of the command line.
End	Moves the cursor to the end of the command line.
Ins	Toggles Insert mode on and off.
Del	Deletes characters.
←	Moves the cursor one character to the left.
→	Moves the cursor one character to the right.
↑	Displays the previous command.
↓	Displays the next command.
Ctrl+←	Moves the cursor to the beginning of a word.
Ctrl+→	Moves the cursor to the beginning of the next word.
Ctrl+End	Deletes from the cursor to the end of the line.
Ctrl+Home	Deletes from the beginning of the line to the cursor.

There are several editing commands you can use only when KEYS is set to off. Function keys F1 through F5 work the same way that the same function keys work at the DOS command line.

F1	Copies one character from the last command.
F2	Displays all the characters in the last command up to the character you type.
F3	Repeats the last command.

F4   Deletes all the characters in the last command up to
        but not including the character you type.

F5   Copies the current command into the buffer and
        clears the command line.

The DOS equivalent of the KEYS command is the DOSKEY command.

• SWITCHES

ON   Turns command-line editing on.

OFF   Turns command-line editing off.

LIST   Displays a list of the commands entered during this
        session, up to a maximum of 64K of characters.

• EXAMPLES

To see the current status of KEYS, type

KEYS

To tell OS/2 to store commands typed at the command prompt, use

KEYS ON

If you want to list the contents of the KEYS memory area, use

KEYS LIST

Use

KEYS OFF

to stop recording commands at the command line.

• NOTES   If you enter KEYS ON, you disable ANSI extended
keyboard support in OS/2 sessions.

See also ANSI, DOSKEY.

LABEL

The LABEL command lets you attach or change the short text description of a disk known as the volume label.

• SYNTAX AND DESCRIPTION

LABEL *drive: text*

The *drive* parameter specifies the drive letter that contains the disk you want to label; if you don't specify a drive letter, the LABEL command defaults to the current drive.

The *text* specifies the text label you want to attach to this disk, up to a total of 11 characters. You can use spaces between words in the label text, but leading spaces will be ignored. You cannot use punctuation characters in a volume label.

Use the LABEL command with no parameters to display the current volume label.

• EXAMPLES

If you want to look at the volume label on drive C, type

LABEL C:

The operating system will then prompt you to enter a new volume label, or to press the Enter key to leave the volume label unchanged.

To change the volume label on drive C to the text *BIG_DISK*, type

LABEL C: BIG_DISK

• NOTES
You can also add a volume label to a disk if you format the disk using the FORMAT command /V switch.

The LABEL command does not work on drives that have an ASSIGN, JOIN, or SUBST command in effect, and LABEL does not work on network drives.

See also FORMAT, VOL.

MAKEINI

The MAKEINI file recreates the OS/2 startup files OS2.INI and OS2SYS.INI.

• SYNTAX AND DESCRIPTION

The MAKEINI file can have two different forms, depending on the file you want to recreate. These are as follows:

MAKEINI OS2.INI

or

MAKEINI OS2SYS.INI

The OS2.INI file contains system settings such as application program defaults, display options, and file options; and the OS2SYS.INI file contains information on fonts and printer drivers.

If you see an OS/2 error message stating that your OS2.INI file is corrupted, you should use the MAKEINI command to recreate both files.

• EXAMPLES

To recreate new OS/2 system and user INI files, follow these steps:

1. Reboot your computer using your original OS/2 Installation disk in drive A.

2. When the OS/2 logo screen appears, remove the Installation disk, insert OS/2 Disk #1 into drive A, and press the Enter key to continue.

3. When the "Welcome to OS/2" screen appears, press the Esc key.

4. Change to the drive where OS/2 is installed on your system, usually drive C, by typing

   C:

5. Change to the OS2 directory by typing

   CD OS2

6. Delete the current INI files as follows:

   DEL OS2.INI
   DEL OS2SYS.INI

7. Use the MAKEINI command as follows to recreate your INI files:

   MAKEINI OS2.INI INI.RC
   MAKEINI OS2SYS.INI INISYS.RC

8. Remove the OS/2 disk from drive A, and reboot your computer.

MD OR MKDIR

The MD command creates a new directory or subdirectory on a disk. MD is an abbreviation for the MKDIR command; you can use either, they both do the same thing.

• SYNTAX AND DESCRIPTION

MD *drive:\path\new directory name*

Both OS/2 and DOS support multiple levels of directories, with the root directory at the top of the whole structure, and directories leading to other directories from the root. The terms *directory* and *subdirectory* are used interchangeably.

The MD command requires you to specify a directory name on the command line. The directory will be created as a subdirectory of the current directory. If you add a backslash before the new name, the directory will be created in the root directory. If you specify complete drive and path information, you can create the new directory on another drive.

Two subdirectories can have the same name, as long as they exist in separate directories. For example, the \LOTUS123 directory can have a subdirectory called \DATA (\LOTUS123\DATA), and so can the \WORD directory (\WORD\DATA).

• EXAMPLES

If you want to create a subdirectory called STUFF in the current directory on the current drive, type

MD STUFF

To create the same subdirectory in the root directory of the current drive, type

MD \STUFF

To create a subdirectory called DATA below the existing directory MYSTUFF on drive B, type

MD B:\MYSTUFF\DATA

You can also create more than one directory at a time if you separate their names with spaces, as follows:

MD C:\ONE C:\TWO

creates two subdirectories in the root directory on drive C.

● **NOTES** See also CD, DIR, RD, TREE.

MEM

 DOS

The MEM command lists the amount of free and used memory in the current DOS session.

● **SYNTAX AND DESCRIPTION**

MEM /switches

The MEM command lists all the memory available to the current DOS session, including high memory, expanded memory, and extended memory. In this respect, MEM differs from the CHKDSK command, which only lists information on conventional memory. MEM is also faster than CHKDSK, because it only reports on memory and does not have to check disk information.

Use MEM with no switches to see a short summary display of memory availability.

● **SWITCHES**

/PROGRAM Displays the programs loaded into memory. This switch can be abbreviated to /P.

/DEBUG Displays the memory and status of programs and device drivers. This switch can be abbreviated to /D.

/CLASSIFY Displays the status of programs loaded into conventional and upper memory. This switch can be abbreviated to /C.

• EXAMPLES

To see a display of the programs loaded into memory and the status of conventional, expanded, and extended memory, use

MEM /P

• NOTES   You can only use one MEM switch at a time; you cannot combine switches.

See also CHKDSK.

MODE

The MODE command lets you configure peripherals attached to your computer system. The command can be used with different types of peripheral device, and it takes different switches depending on the circumstances. For the sake of clarity, in the discussions that follow the MODE command's functions are separated into several subentries.

MODE (COMMUNICATIONS)

The MODE command sets asynchronous communications parameters for DOS and OS/2 sessions.

• SYNTAX AND DESCRIPTION

MODE *COMn* *baud, parity, databits, stopbits, P, handshake*

Before using the MODE command to establish communication port settings, make sure that the appropriate device driver is loaded in CONFIG.SYS.

COMn   Specifies the number of the serial port from COM1: through COM4:.

baud   Sets the baud rate. If the port does not support direct memory access (DMA), choose from 110, 150, 300, 600, 1200, 1800, 2400, 3600, 4800, 7200, 9600, 19200, 38400, and 57600. For ports that do support DMA, choose from 300, 600, 1200, 2400, 4800, 9600, 19200, 38400, 57600, 76800, 115200, 138240, 172800, 230400, or 345600. If you do not specify a rate, the default of 1200 will be used.

parity   Specifies the parity. Select N (none), O (odd), E (even), M (mark), or S (space). The default is E.

databits   Specifies the number of data bits in each word. Choose from 5, 6, 7, or 8. The default is 7.

stopbits   Specifies the number of stop bits. Choose from 1, 1.5, or 2. The default is 2 when the baud rate is 110; otherwise the default is 1.

P   Specifies a 30-second timeout for DOS programs that write directly to the hardware. This parameter is only available in DOS sessions.

The *parity*, *databits*, *stopbits*, and *P* parameters must be specified in the order listed above. If a parameter is not specified, include a comma in its place. If the number of *stopbits* is set to 1.5, the number of *databits* must be set to 5.

In an OS/2 session, the MODE command can also set several additional parameters designated by the *handshake* option in the syntax line shown above. Many of these parameters allow you to control low-level communications hardware functions, as follows:

TO   Specifies the type of timeout. TO=ON allows for an infinite timeout; TO=OFF, the default, allows for a 60-second timeout.

XON   XON=ON sets automatic transmit flow control; the default is XON=OFF.

IDSR	IDSR=ON sets input handshaking using data set ready (DSR), the default. IDSR=OFF turns off data-set-ready handshaking.
ODSR	ODSR=ON sets output handshaking using data set ready (DSR), the default. ODSR=OFF turns off data-set-ready handshaking.
OCTS	OCTS=ON sets output handshaking using clear to send (CTS), the default. OCTS=OFF turns off clear-to-send handshaking.
DTR	DTR=ON sets data terminal ready (DTR), the default. DTR=OFF prevents DTR, and DTR=HS allows input handshaking using DTR.
RTS	RTS=ON sets request to send (RTS), the default. RTS=OFF prevents RTS, RTS=HS allows input handshaking using RTS, and RTS=TOG allows RTS toggling in transmit mode.
BUFFER	Sets extended hardware buffering. Choose from ON, OFF, and AUTO.
ENHANCED	Enables or disables enhanced mode support provided by the hardware on the communications port. In enhanced mode, processing is performed in either first in first out (FIFO) mode, or in direct memory access (DMA) mode.
RXDMA	Controls the DMA receive operations and can be set to AUTO, OFF, or ON.
TXDMA	Controls the DMA transmit operations and can be set to AUTO, ON, or OFF.

• EXAMPLES

To see the status of the asynchronous COM 1 port, type

MODE COM1:

To set COM1: baud rate, parity, data bits and stop bits, use

MODE COM1: 9600, N, 8, 1

separating each parameter by a comma.

If you don't want to reset all the parameters, use a comma in place of the default you want to keep:

MODE COM1:9600,,,,,

• NOTES The P parameter does not provide for an infinite number of retries as it does in MS-DOS 5.

MODE (VIDEO)

The MODE command can also control the video output to one or more monitors.

• SYNTAX AND DESCRIPTION

MODE *CON# display, rows*

CON#   Specifies the display number, either CON1 or CON2.

display   Sets the display mode: 40, 80, or 132 columns; BW40, BW80, BW132 for black & white monitors; CO40, CO80, or CO132 for color monitors; and MONO for monochrome monitors.

rows   Sets the number of rows, 25, 43, or 50, depending on the video adapter installed in your computer.

• EXAMPLES

To set a color 80 column by 43 row display on display number 1, type

MODE CON1 CO80, 43

Always separate the display parameter from the rows parameter by a comma.

MODE (PRINTER)

The MODE command can set parallel printer parameters.

• SYNTAX AND DESCRIPTION

MODE *number* *characters*, *lines*, *P*

number	Specifies the printer number, LPT1, LPT2, or LPT3. PRN is also an acceptable entry for this parameter. MODE also supports LPT4 through LPT9 for network printers.
characters	Sets the number of characters per line, either 80 (the default) or 132.
lines	Sets the number of lines per vertical inch, either 6 (the default), or 8.
P	Tells the MODE command to continue to output to the printer even if a timeout occurs.

• EXAMPLES

To set up your printer as LPT1 with 132 characters across the page and 6 lines per inch, type

MODE LPT1 132,6

Always separate the characters parameter from the lines parameter by a comma.

MODE (DISK WRITE VERIFICATION)

The MODE command also turns on or off disk write verification.

• SYNTAX AND DESCRIPTION

MODE *DSKT* *VER=state*

where *state* is either ON or OFF.

• EXAMPLES

To turn disk write verification on, type

MODE DSKT VER=ON

MORE

The MORE command displays information one screen at a time, instead of scrolling continuously.

• SYNTAX AND DESCRIPTION

command | **MORE**

where *command* is the command (including parameters if appropriate) whose output you want to display one screen at a time. When the screen is full, you will see the prompt

-- MORE --

on the last screen line. Press any key to see the next 24 lines of output. The | symbol above represents a pipe.

The MORE command can also take input from a file, as in the following syntax:

MORE *<path\filename*

where the < character is a redirection symbol.

MORE is considered to be a special type of command called a *filter;* the FIND and SORT commands are also filters.

• EXAMPLES

To pause the output when typing the README file, use

TYPE README | MORE

An alternative way of producing the same result is to type

MORE < README

• **NOTES**   You can use Ctrl+Break at the **-- More --** prompt to cancel the MORE command and return to the command processor.

Be careful when using the MORE command in a window, you may not be able to see all the output, depending on the size of your window.

See also FIND, SORT.

MOVE

The MOVE command moves files from one directory to another directory on the same drive.

• SYNTAX AND DESCRIPTION

MOVE *drive:\path1**filename1*** *path2\filename2*

where *path1\filename1* specifies the file you want to move, and *path2\filename2* specifies the new file name and location.

The MOVE command only works when both the source and the target directories are on the same disk. If you don't specify a target directory, the file or files will be moved into the current directory.

154   OS/2 Commands

You can use the wildcard characters * and ? in either the source or the target files if you wish. Also, if you specify a new file name and extension you can move the file and rename it at the same time.

• EXAMPLES

To move MYFILE.TXT into the WORD directory, type

MOVE MYFILE.TXT \WORD

To move all the files with the file-name extenion .DOC into the WORD directory, use

MOVE *.DOC \WORD

To move a file called CHAPTER1 into a directory called BOOK and rename the file CHAPTER2, type

MOVE CHAPTER1 \BOOK\CHAPTER2

• NOTES   See also COPY, REN.

PATCH

The PATCH command lets you make IBM-supplied changes or patches to existing software. Most people will never need to use this command. You should only use it when you understand *exactly* what you are doing when you change the contents of an executable file. It only takes one error to make a program completely unusable.

• SYNTAX AND DESCRIPTION

PATCH *path\filename /A*

path\filename specifies the name and path of the file you want to patch. If you are implementing an IBM-supplied patch, add the /A switch and the patch will be applied and verified automatically.

If you do not specify the /A switch, PATCH guides you through the whole process interactively. First, you are asked to provide a hexadecimal offset to indicate where the patch should be made. PATCH displays the contents of the 16 bytes associated with that location with the cursor positioned on the first byte. You can enter one or two hexadecimal digits to change the contents of this byte, or use the spacebar to leave this byte unchanged and move on to the next byte. Patching continues until you press the Enter key, then OS/2 asks if you want to continue. Press Y (yes) to continue, and PATCH prompts you for another offset. When all the patches have been entered, OS/2 displays them on your screen and asks if they should be applied. If you answer yes, they are written to the disk file in the order in which they were entered.

If you answer no, you can correct any mistakes before continuing.

• SWITCHES

/A   Tells the PATCH command to patch the file automatically; if /A is omitted, the file will be patched interactively.

• EXAMPLES

To interactively apply a patch to the file OS2PROG.EXE, type

PATCH OS2PROG.EXE

• NOTES   All offsets and patches must be entered in hexadecimal.

PICVIEW

The PICVIEW command lets you display a picture file.

• SYNTAX AND DESCRIPTION

To start PICVIEW from the OS/2 command prompt, use the following:

PICVIEW *path\filename /switches*

path\filename specifies the path and file-name information for the picture file you want to display.

If you type PICVIEW with no parameters, the Picture Viewer window opens; select a file to view using the Open selection from the File menu. If you type PICVIEW followed by a file name, the Picture Viewer window opens displaying the specified file.

You can also start PICVIEW if you select the Picture Viewer from inside the OS/2 Productivity folder.

• SWITCHES

/MET   Specifies that the file you want to view is a metafile. A metafile is a special kind of graphics file that contains not only the image, but also instructions on how the image should be displayed. This allows the image to be output to a variety of different devices. Metafiles always have the file-name extension .MET.

/PIF   Specifies that the file you want to view is a picture interchange file (PIF), a type of file format used in exchanging images between applications. Picture interchange files always have the file-name extension .PIF.

/P   Tells PICVIEW to print the selected file.

/S   Specifies that the Picture Viewer should return to
           its default screen position.

• EXAMPLES

To view a metafile called ELVIS.MET, type

PICVIEW ELVIS /MET

If you want to print the file, add

PICVIEW ELVIS /MET /P

• **NOTES**   You can also display spool files by using PICVIEW.
OS/2 spool files always have the file-name extension .SPL.

PMREXX

The PMREXX command provides a windowed environment used to
display output from REXX procedures and to accept input to them.

• SYNTAX AND DESCRIPTION

PMREXX *path\filename arguments*

where *path\filename* specifies the name of the .CMD file to be displayed, and *arguments* specifies the arguments used in the REXX
program.

REXX is a complex programming language built into OS/2 you can
use to create procedures that replace traditional batch programs.

When you start PMREXX, you add several important features to
REXX, including

- A window to display the output from REXX procedures

- An input window for REXX procedures

- A browsing, scrolling, and clipboard capability for REXX

- A set of fonts for use in the output window

- A window used for testing REXX procedures with the
  REXXTRY.CMD program

• EXAMPLES

To display the current PATH statement in a CONFIG.SYS file referenced by the REXX program MYPROG.CMD, type

PMREXX MYPROG PATH

PRINT

The PRINT command prints the specified file.

• SYNTAX AND DESCRIPTION

PRINT *drive:\path***filename** */switches*

The PRINT command prints or cancels the printing of one or more
files. You can use the wildcard characters * and ? to specify the
printing of several files in a directory, and the files are queued
for printing in the order that you specify them.

• SWITCHES

/D:*device* Specifies the printing device name; the default is LPT1. Acceptable names are PRN, LPT1 through LPT3, and if you are using a network printer, LPT4 through LPT9. This switch must be the first switch on the command line.

/B Prevents Ctrl+Z characters being interpreted as end-of-file markers and interrupting printing. The entire file is printed.

/C Cancels the file now printing if spooling is active. This switch is only available in OS/2 sessions.

/T Cancels all printing if spooling is active. This switch is only available in OS/2 sessions.

• EXAMPLES

To print the file in the current directory called MYFILE.TXT on the default printer, LPT1, type

PRINT MYFILE.TXT

To cancel the printing of the current file, use

PRINT /C

and to cancel the file currently being printed and all the other files in the print queue, type

PRINT /T

• **NOTES** The DOS and OS/2 PRINT commands do not use exactly the same switches. The DOS /M, /S, and /U switches, used to specify how long DOS should wait for the printer, are not available under OS/2.

Also, under DOS the /B: switch sets the size of the internal print buffer; under OS/2, this is controlled by PRINTMONBUFSIZE rather than by a PRINT switch. Under OS/2, /B (with no :) stops PRINT from processing Ctrl+Z characters as the end-of-file marker.

The OS/2 switches /C and /T are not available under MS-DOS 5.

Do not use the /C and /T switches together with a file name, or with the /B switch.

See also SPOOL.

PROMPT

The PROMPT command changes the system command prompt.

• SYNTAX AND DESCRIPTION

PROMPT *text*

Typing PROMPT without a parameter resets the prompt to the appropriate default. OS/2 and DOS system prompts are independent; changing one does not change the other.

The default OS/2 command prompt is the name of the current directory contained in square brackets. For example, if the OS2 directory on drive C is your current directory, your prompt will look like this:

[C:\OS2]

The default DOS system prompt is the current drive letter, followed by the > symbol. If you are in the OS2 directory on drive C, you command prompt will look like this:

C:>

You can specify a custom system prompt, consisting of any text you want, and the operating system will display it as the system prompt.

The PROMPT command can contain any of the following special characters when preceded by a $ sign:

Command	Special Character
A	& symbol
B	| symbol
C	(symbol
D	Current date
E	An escape character (ASCII 27)
F	) symbol
G	> symbol
H	Backspace
I	The help line
L	< symbol
N	Current drive letter
P	Current directory of the default drive
Q	= symbol
R	Return code or error level
S	Space
T	Current system time
V	The operating system version number
_(underscore)	Adds carriage-return and line-feed characters for a multiline prompt
$	$ symbol

• EXAMPLES

To set the system prompt to display **Good Morning** followed by the name of the current directory, type

PROMPT Good Morning $P

A common DOS prompt includes the name of the current directory, followed by the > symbol. To set this prompt, type

PROMPT PG

• **NOTES**   If you use PROMPT $V in either an OS/2 session or in a DOS session to display the operating system version number, the OS/2 version number is displayed in both prompts. The DOS version number is never displayed.

The system command prompt can be set using the SET command, or you can establish a prompt in CONFIG.SYS.

See also DATE, HELP, SET, TIME, VER.

PSTAT

The PSTAT command gives you information on processes, threads, priority levels, system semaphores, shared memory, and dynamic library links.

• SYNTAX AND DESCRIPTION

PSTAT /switches

Use the PSTAT command with no switches to see information about current processes and threads, system semaphores, shared memory, and dynamic link libraries.

• SWITCHES

/C   Displays current process and thread information, including, for each process, the process ID number, parent process ID number, session ID number, and process name.

            For each thread, the following is displayed: thread ID number, state, priority, and block ID number

/S   Displays semaphore information for each thread, including process module name and ID number, session ID number, index number, number of references, number of requests, flag number, and semaphore name.

/L   Displays a list of the dynamic link libraries for each process, including process module name and ID number, session ID number, and library list.

/M   Displays shared memory information for each process, including handle number, selector number, number of references, and shared memory name.

/P:*id*   Displays information about the specified process, including process ID number, parent process ID number, session ID number, process module name, a list of dynamic link libraries, and shared memory name. For each thread, the following information is displayed: thread ID number, priority number, status, block ID, and owned semaphore information.

• EXAMPLES

To display information on the current processes and threads in your system, type

PSTAT /C

If you want to look at semaphore information for each thread, type

PSTAT /S

To see information about a particular process, first determine the process ID number using

PSTAT /C

Then enter the ID number after the /P switch. For example, if the ID number is 0002, use this number as follows:

PSTAT /P:0002

• NOTES   Depending on the current state of your system, the PSTAT command can generate a large amount of information, several screens full, so it is a good idea to make PSTAT display the information one screen at a time by adding a pipe to the MORE command, as follows:

PSTAT */switches* | **MORE**

RD OR RMDIR

The RD command removes the specified directory as long as the directory is empty. RD is an abbreviation for RMDIR; you can use either command, both do the same thing.

• SYNTAX AND DESCRIPTION

RD *drive:\path*

You must delete all files from a directory before you can remove the directory from your system. If a directory contains subdirectories, you must first delete all the files in the subdirectories, then you can remove the subdirectories followed by the parent directory.

In an OS/2 session you can remove several empty directories at the same time.

• EXAMPLES

To remove the DATA subdirectory from the LOTUS123 directory on the current drive, first use the DEL command to erase all the files in DATA, then type

RD DATA

to remove the directory.

In an OS/2 session you can remove several directories with just one RD command. To remove the empty PROGRAMS subdirectory from the CLIB directory and the empty ELVIS directory from the ROCKSTAR directory, type

RD \CLIB\PROGRAMS \ROCKSTAR\ELVIS

• **NOTES**   You cannot remove the root directory, nor can you remove the current directory. In a DOS session you cannot remove directories affected by a JOIN or a SUBST command.

RECOVER

The RECOVER command rescues files from a disk that has bad sectors.

• SYNTAX AND DESCRIPTION

RECOVER *drive:\path**filename***

or

RECOVER *drive:*

The RECOVER command recovers data from a file on a disk with bad sectors, or reconstructs all the files on a disk with a corrupted directory structure. You can use RECOVER to retrieve those portions of a file that can still be read, but it is important to remember that no data is recovered from the bad sectors themselves. RECOVER can only recover those portions of the file stored in the readable sectors on the disk; the other information is lost forever. For this reason, there is absolutely no point in running the RECOVER command on program files, because the program will never run correctly if a chunk of the file is missing. It is sometimes worth using RECOVER on long text files.

In the first syntax above, *drive:* specifies the drive that contains the file you want to recover; in the second syntax, it specifies that the entire drive is to be recovered. *path\filename* specifies the file you want to recover.

RECOVER saves what information it can from the damaged files and stores the results in consecutive files beginning with FILE0001.REC. Any HPFS extended attributes are saved in consecutively numbered files named EA0000.REC. By recovering the files, the structure of the disk is rebuilt from scratch. You now have to examine these files one by one to see what, if anything, can be salvaged.

Because the RECOVER command locks the disk it is working on so that no other processes can access the disk at the same time, you cannot recover the disk that contains the RECOVER command, or the boot disk used to start OS/2.

To recover files on the drive that you use to start OS/2, follow these steps:

1. Copy the files C:\OS2\RECOVER.COM and C:\OS2\ SYSTEM\OSO001.MSG onto a blank formatted disk.

2. Insert the OS/2 Installation disk in drive A and reboot your computer.

3. At the [A:\] command prompt, type the following commands:

    SETDPATH=A:
    SETPATH=A:

These commands make sure that OS/2 is running from drive A.

4. Remove the Installation disk from drive A and insert the disk onto which you copied RECOVER.COM and OSO001.MSG.

5. Type the following command:

    RECOVER *C:filename*

• EXAMPLES

To recover a file in the root directory of drive B called MYFILE.TXT, type

RECOVER A:\MYFILE.TXT

If you want to recover all the files on drive A because the directory structure is damaged, type

RECOVER A:

• NOTES   If you are using the HPFS, make sure you use the
RECOVER command from an OS/2 session so that any extended attributes will be saved properly.

Also, when RECOVER is run on a disk containing the HPFS, files are recovered, but not the entire disk. RECOVER initially attempts to use the original file name, but if this is impossible, it uses the convention FILE*nnnn*.REC. A damaged sector in the middle of a file will be filled with zeros in the recovered file to preserve the original file size.

The RECOVER command cannot work on drives with ASSIGN, JOIN, or SUBST commands in effect, and the command does not work on network drives.

See also CHKDSK.

REN OR RENAME

The REN command changes a file's name or extension. REN is short for RENAME; you can use either command, they both do the same thing. In an OS/2 session, you can also change the name of a directory.

• SYNTAX AND DESCRIPTION

REN *drive:\path***oldname newname**

The *oldname* specifies the file to be renamed, while *newname* specifies the new filename. The name may also be the name of a directory that you want to change.

You cannot specify a drive and path name in *newname*; therefore the file stays in the same directory after the name is changed.

• EXAMPLES

To change the name of a file in the current directory called BUDGET92 to BUDGET 93, type

REN BUDGET92 BUDGET93

To change all the file-name extensions in the current directory from .LVS to .ELL, type

REN *.LVS *.ELL

• **NOTES**   You can use the wildcard characters * or ? if you wish when renaming files but not when renaming directories.

See also COPY, MOVE.

REPLACE

The REPLACE command replaces files on the target drive with files of the same name copied from the source drive. REPLACE can also selectively copy files from the source drive to the target drive.

• SYNTAX AND DESCRIPTION

REPLACE *sourcedrive:\path**filename targetdrive:**\path /switches*

In the REPLACE command *filename* specifies the file to be copied from the source drive that will replace a file of the same name on the target.

You can use the wildcard characters * and ? in file names or extensions; however, hidden and system files are not copied if you use the *.* method of specifying all files.

• SWITCHES

/A   Copies all the files from the source drive that do not exist on the target drive.

/S   Updates those files that already exist on the target with new copies from the source.

/P   Prompts you as each file is found on the target drive, allowing you to control the process and selectively add or not add files as you wish.

/R   Replaces read-only files on the target drive.

/W   Waits for you to insert a floppy disk before starting to search for the source files.

/U   Only updates files on the target drive that are older than those on the source drive.

/F   Halts the REPLACE command if the source file
        contains HPFS extended attributes and the target disk
        cannot support extended attributes.

• EXAMPLES

To replace the MEMO file on drive B with a copy of MEMO from
drive C, type

REPLACE C:MEMO B:

If you want to copy all the files from the current directory that do
not exist on drive A without overwriting existing files, type

REPLACE C:*.* A: /A

• **NOTES**   You cannot use the /A switch (prevents the overwriting of existing files) in combination with the /S or /U switches
(requires the overwriting of existing files).

See also BACKUP, COPY, MOVE, XCOPY.

RESTORE

The RESTORE command reloads files that were made using the
BACKUP command. You can use the RESTORE command to reload
backed up files after a hard disk problem; you can also use BACK-
UP and RESTORE to move a file or set of files from one computer to
another.

• SYNTAX AND DESCRIPTION

RESTORE *source drive:* *target drive:\path\filename /switches*

In the RESTORE command *source drive* indicates the drive letter
containing the files that you previously backed up, and *target drive*
specifies the location to which you want to restore those files. RE-
STORE only works with files originally created using the BACKUP
command, and restores files to the directories in which they were
originally located. If you have several floppy disks to restore, you
must load them in the same order that they were created. You can
use the wildcard characters * and ? with RESTORE if you wish.

• SWITCHES

/P	Asks your permission before restoring read-only files, or files that have changed since the last backup was made.
/M	Restores only those files on the target disk that have changed since the last backup was made.
/B:*mm-dd-yy*	Restores only those files on the target disk that were modified on or before the specified date.
/A:*mm-dd-yy*	Restores only those files on the target disk that were modified at or on or after the specified date.
/E:*hh:mm:ss*	Restores only those files on the target disk that were modified before the specified time.
/L:*hh:mm:ss*	Restores only those files on the target disk that were modified at or after the specified time.
/S	Restores files and subdirectories. If you do not specify this switch, the RESTORE command only works within the source directory.
/N	Restores files that do not exist on the target disk.
/F	Stops the RESTORE command if the target disk cannot support the HPFS extended attributes present on the source disk.

/D   Lists all the files on the backup disk that match file names on the target disk, but without restoring any files.

• EXAMPLES

To rebuild all the files on drive C using a set of backup disks loaded on drive A, type

RESTORE A: C:*.* /S

If you just want to restore a single file, MYFILE.TXT, from drive A, type

RESTORE A: C:MYFILE.TXT

To list the files on the backup disk that match files on the target disk, but not restore any files, type

RESTORE /D

• NOTES The RESTORE command does not restore COM-MAND.COM and CMD.EXE, or any of the OS/2 or DOS hidden files normally found in the root directory. This means that you cannot use RESTORE to create a bootable hard or floppy disk.

Do not use RESTORE with a drive affected by an ASSIGN, JOIN, or SUBST command.

See also ATTRIB, RESTORE, XCOPY.

SETBOOT

The SETBOOT command lets you set up the Boot Manager for your hard disk.

• SYNTAX AND DESCRIPTION

SETBOOT */switches*

• SWITCHES

/T:*x*	Specifies the length of time that the Boot Manager menu will stay on the screen, in seconds, before the default system starts running. A value of 0 seconds bypasses this menu and starts the default system running immediately.
/T:NO	Leaves the Boot Manager menu on the screen until you make a selection.
/M:*m*	Specifies the mode for the startup menu:

> *m* = n for normal mode
>
> *m* = a for advanced mode

/Q	Queries the current startup environment, and displays the default logical disk alias, timeout value, mode, and drive letter assignments for unattended operation.
/B	Performs an orderly shutdown of the system and then restarts the system again.
/X:*x*	Sets the system startup index to the appropriate partition number, where *x* is from 0 to 3.
/O:*name*	Establishes the partition or logical drive specified in *name* as the operating system to be booted.

• EXAMPLES

To disable the startup selection time, type

SETBOOT /T:NO

To put the Boot Manager into advanced mode, type

SETBOOT /M:a

To display detail of the current startup environment, use

SETBOOT /Q

● **NOTES**   See also FDISK, FDISKPM.

SORT

The SORT command rearranges the contents of ASCII text files. It can also take input from a command, or a device, and output sorted lines of text to a file or a device.

● SYNTAX AND DESCRIPTION

SORT */R /+column*

The SORT command usually sorts from A to Z, then from 0 through 9, although you can reverse this order with a switch if you wish. SORT does not differentiate between uppercase and lowercase letters, and it sorts characters above ASCII 127 based on rules derived from the currently active COUNTRY code.

SORT is a filter command and usually takes its input from a pipe, a redirected file, or a device, and then sorts that input. There are two ways to use SORT:

● To sort the contents of a data file, type **SORT**, the redirection symbol for input (<), and then the name of the file you want to sort. Do not use any wildcard characters in the file name. SORT will read the file you specified, sort the contents, and display the result. This command might look like this:

SORT < MYFILE.TXT

● To sort the output of a command, type the command along with any parameters or switches, then the redirection

symbol for a pipe (|), and then the SORT command. This
command might look like this if you use the DIR command:

DIR | SORT

• SWITCHES

/R   Reverses the normal sort order to sort from
                  Z to A, then from 9 to 0.

/+*column*   SORT usually takes the character in
                  column 1 as the basis for sorting; however,
                  you can specify that the character in *column*
                  number column be used instead.

• EXAMPLES

To sort the contents of a file called CHAPTER.ONE into reverse
order and store the result in a file called REVISE.ONE, type

SORT /R < CHAPTER.ONE > REVISE.ONE

To sort the contents of the current directory into alphabetical order by
file name, and display the resulting list on the screen one screen at a
time, you can combine the SORT and the MORE filters, as follows:

DIR | SORT | MORE

• NOTES   The SORT command is one of a group of special
programs called filters; the FIND and MORE commands are also
filters.

The OS/2 SORT command does not work with files larger than 63K
(64,512 bytes).

See also FIND, MORE.

SPOOL

The SPOOL command redirects printer output from one device to another.

• SYNTAX AND DESCRIPTION

SPOOL /switches

The SPOOL command can redirect printer output from one parallel printer to another, or from a parallel printer to a serial printer. Use the command with no switches to start SPOOL running or to see the current status of SPOOL and information on current printer assignments.

• SWITCHES

/D:*device*   Specifies the input device used by application programs for printing. Valid device names are LPT1 (the default name), LPT2, LPT3, and PRN. Serial COM# devices cannot be specified as input devices.

/O:*device*   Specifies the output print device. Valid *device* names are LPT1, LPT2, LPT3, and PRN, or COM1 through COM4. The default is the same as your choice for /D:*device*.

/Q   Displays current device redirections. The default setup has each input device assign to the corresponding output device; LPT1 is directed to LPT1, LPT2 to LPT2, and so on.

• EXAMPLES

To start the spooler, type

SPOOL

If you want to redirect output from LPT1 to LPT3, use the following:

SPOOL /O:LPT1 /O:LPT3

• **NOTES**   If you want to spool to a serial printer, you must add a DEVICE statement in your CONFIG.SYS file for the COM.SYS device driver. Use the MODE command to make sure that the serial port is configured correctly for your serial printer.

Some DOS programs do not contain the appropriate instructions to work correctly with the spooler, and you may find that a print file will not be printed until you close the application program. To fix this problem and force printer output, press the Ctrl, Alt, and PrtSc keys together. This causes the temporary spool file to close and print.

See also DEVICE, MODE, PRINT.

START

The START command starts an OS/2 program in another OS/2 session.

• SYNTAX AND DESCRIPTION

START *"program" /switches command command_inputs*

Type this command with no switches to start a new OS/2 session. To load a program in a new OS/2 session, use START followed by a name enclosed in quotes (no longer than 60 characters) and the appropriate switches. This name will be displayed in the OS/2 window list and at the top of the program window. *command* can specify any OS/2 command, batch program, or application program, and *command_inputs* represents any arguments needed for the *command*.

• SWITCHES

/K	Starts the program using CMD.EXE and keeps the session running when the program ends.
/C	Starts the program using CMD.EXE and closes the session when the program ends.
/N	Starts the program directly without invoking CMD.EXE. You cannot use this switch to start a batch file or an internal OS/2 command. Do not enclose the program title in quotation marks.
/F	Starts the program running in the foreground.
/B	Starts the program running in the background.
/PGM"*name*"	Interprets the "*name*" string as containing the name of the program.
/FS	Indicates that the application is a full-screen DOS or OS/2 application that must run in a separate session.
/WIN	Indicates that the application is an OS/2 application that runs within an OS/2 or DOS window.
/PM	Indicates that the application is a Program Manager application.
/DOS	Starts the program as a DOS program.
/MAX	Asks that a windowed application starts in a maximized window.
/MIN	Asks that a windowed application starts as an icon in a minimized state.

/I   Forces the new session to inherit the
                      environment variables established by SET
                      commands in the CONFIG.SYS file, instead
                      of the CMD.EXE environment variables of
                      the current session.

• EXAMPLES

To begin a new OS/2 session from the command prompt, type

START

To start a new DOS session, use

START /DOS

• **NOTES**   Several of the START switches are mutually ex-
clusive. Choose one switch from the group /K, /C, and /N, one from
/F and /B, one from the group /FS, /WIN, /PM, /DOS, and one
from /MAX and /MIN.

SUBST

The SUBST command substitutes a drive letter for a complete drive
and path name to simplify access to long and complex paths.

• SYNTAX AND DESCRIPTION

SUBST *newdrive: existing drive:\path /switches*

Drive and path combinations can often get very long and complex.
SUBST offers a way around this problem by using a drive letter instead of a long complex path. In the SUBST command, *newdrive:*
specifies the drive letter you want to use instead of the *existing*

drive:\path path. The *newdrive:* must be an unused drive letter; you cannot use a drive letter that already exists on your system.

Type SUBST with no parameters to see a list of the currently substituted drives.

• SWITCHES

/D   Removes a drive and path substitution.

• EXAMPLES

To substitute the drive letter H for the path C:\OS2\PROGS \MYPROGS, type

SUBST H: C:\OS2\PROGS\MYPROGS

Now you can type

DIR H

instead of the cumbersome

DIR C:\OS2\PROGS\MYPROGS

• **NOTES**   The following commands do not work in DOS sessions on drives that have a SUBST command in effect: BACKUP, CHKDSK, DISKCOMP, DISKCOPY, FORMAT, LABEL, RECOVER, RESTORE.

See also ASSIGN, JOIN.

SYSLEVEL

The SYSLEVEL command displays the OS/2 operating system service level.

• SYNTAX AND DESCRIPTION

SYSLEVEL

The SYSLEVEL command displays the name of the directory that contains SYSLEVEL data, the name and revision level of the operating system, and the current and prior corrective service levels.

• EXAMPLES

To display OS/2 revision-level information, type

SYSLEVEL

SYSLOG

OS/2

The SYSLOG command lets you look at or print the contents of the system error-log file. SYSLOG also turns error logging on or off.

• SYNTAX AND DESCRIPTION

SYSLOG *switches*

To use the SYSLOG command, you must have the following statements in your CONFIG.SYS file:

DEVICE = C:\OS2\LOG.SYS
RUN = C:\OS2\SYSTEM\LOGDAEM.EXE

assuming your OS/2 system was installed on drive C.

If you type SYSLOG with no parameters, a windowing program opens that tracks system errors. You can use the menu selections in this program to manage your error logging, rather than using command-line switches.

SYSLOG saves error information into a file called LOG0001.DAT, unless you specify a different file name. The error log file is of a fixed size, so that at some point new entries will overwrite existing entries, starting with the oldest; this is known as "wrapping."

• SWITCHES

/S	Suspends error logging.
/R	Restarts error logging.
/P:*filename*	Redirects error logging to the specified path and file name.
/W:*x*	Specifies the size of the error-log file; the default is 64K, the minimum is 4K.

• EXAMPLES

To run the SYSLOG program, type

SYSLOG

To suspend error logging, use

SYSLOG /S

To send error-log information to a file called ERROR.LOG in the directory C:\OS2\SYSTEM, type

SYSLOG /P: C:\OS2\SYSTEM\ERROR.LOG

and to specify a size for this log file of 48K, use

SYSLOG /P: C:\OS2\SYSTEM\ERROR.LOG /W:48

• NOTES   See also DEVICE and RUN in Part VI, "CONFIG.SYS Commands."

TIME

The TIME command displays or resets the system time. Special circuitry inside your computer automatically keeps track of the time, even when the computer is turned off, so it is not usually necessary to reset the time.

• SYNTAX AND DESCRIPTION

TIME *hh:mm:ss:cc*

In the TIME command *hh* specifies the hours, from 0 to 23; *mm* specifies the minutes, from 0 to 59; *ss* specifies the seconds, from 0 to 59; *cc* specifies the hundredths of seconds, from 0 to 99. Hours, minutes, seconds and hundredths are usually separated by periods or colons. You can use the COUNTRY command in your CONFIG.SYS file to change to different separator characters.

Use the TIME command with no parameters to see a display of the current system time on your computer.

• EXAMPLES

To see the current system time on your computer, type

TIME

Type the following to reset the time to 6 p.m.:

TIME 18:00

• NOTES   See also DATE, PROMPT.

TREE

| OS/2 | | DOS |

The TREE command displays all the directories on the specified drive, and optionally lists all the files in these directories.

• SYNTAX AND DESCRIPTION

TREE *drive: /switches*

To see a list of all the directories on the current drive, use the TREE command with no parameters. Add a drive letter to see the directory list for the specified drive. To see both directories and file names, add the /F switch.

• SWITCHES

/F   Lists the names of all files in the root directory and in all subdirectories.

• EXAMPLES

To see a list of all the directories on the current drive, type

TREE

To list all directories and all files on the disk in drive A, type

TREE A: /F

• NOTES   See also CD, DIR, MD, and RD.

TYPE

The TYPE command displays the contents of one or more files on the screen.

• SYNTAX AND DESCRIPTION

TYPE *drive:\path***filename**

The TYPE command will display the contents of any specified file, but is best suited to displaying ASCII files; other file types may be unreadable.

In a DOS session you can type just one file at a time, but in an OS/2 session, you can type multiple files; you can even use the wildcard characters * and ? if you wish.

• EXAMPLES

To display the contents of the file MYFILE.TXT in the C:\DATA directory, type

TYPE C:\DATA\MYFILE.TXT

In an OS/2 session, to display the contents of the files CHAP-TER1.DOC, CHAPTER2.DOC, and CHAPTER3.DOC in the current directory, use

TYPE CHAPTER1.DOC CHAPTER2.DOC CHAPTER3.DOC

The files are displayed in sequence, and each file name is displayed before the contents are displayed.

• NOTES   See also PRINT.

UNDELETE

The UNDELETE command recovers deleted files.

• SYNTAX AND DESCRIPTION

UNDELETE *drive:\path\filename/switches*

You can use the UNDELETE command to recover the deleted file called *filename.* If you do not specify a file name, all the deleted files in the current directory will be restored.

But before you can use UNDELETE to recover deleted files, you must have a DELDIR command in your CONFIG.SYS file for each drive you want to protect, as follows:

SET DELDIR = *driven:\path, maxsize*

DELDIR establishes a directory for each specified drive, into which files are copied when you delete them. In other words, files are not deleted immediately, but instead are copied into this special directory from which they can be recovered by UNDELETE.

Files are only removed from this special directory on an as-needed basis, when the number of deleted files in the directory exceeds the maximum size of the directory. Files are then removed in first in, first out sequence.

Using UNDELETE is fine for recovering a few files deleted by accident, but it is no substitute for a well thought out, comprehensive backup program.

• SWITCHES

/L   Lists files that could be recovered but does not undelete any files.

/S   Includes all files in the specified directory and all
       subdirectories.

/A   Recovers all available deleted files without waiting
       for confirmation.

/F   Specifies that a file or files be permanently deleted so
       that they cannot be recovered.

• EXAMPLES

To display a list of all files from the current directory available for
recovery, use

UNDELETE /L

To wipe out the file MYFILE.TXT so that it can never be recovered,
type

UNDELETE MYFILE.TXT /F

• **NOTES**   See also the BACKUP, DEL, and RESTORE entries
in this section, and the DELDIR entry in Part VI, "CONFIG.SYS
Commands."

UNPACK

The UNPACK command decompresses compressed files and
copies files from the OS/2 Installation disks. Compressed files have
an @ character as the last character of their file-name extension.

• SYNTAX AND DESCRIPTION

The UNPACK command uses two different syntaxes:

UNPACK *sourcedrive:\path***filename** *targetdrive:***path**
/switches

or

UNPACK *sourcedrive:\path***filename** */SHOW*

To copy a compressed file, specify the drive, path, and file name of
the compressed file, then specify the drive and path where you
want to copy the file, adding switches as needed.

Alternatively, because a packed file can actually contain several
other files, you can use the /SHOW option to list all the files contained inside a packed file.

• SWITCHES

/V	Verifies that the unpacked files were written to disk correctly. This option will make UNPACK run slightly slower as the check is performed for each file.
/F	Tells UNPACK not to unpack files with HPFS extended attributes if the target file system cannot support extended attributes.
/N:*filename*	Specifies that one particular file be unpacked from a packed file containing multiple compressed files.
/SHOW	Lists the target path and file name information for all the compressed files contained inside a packed file.

• EXAMPLES

To unpack all the files contained inside the file called BIGFILE.CO@
in drive A into the OS2 directory on drive C, type

UNPACK A:BIGFILE.CO@ C:\OS2

To display the path and file-name information for all the compressed files contained inside BIGFILE.CO@, type

UNPACK A:BIGFILE.CO@ /SHOW

• **NOTES**   It is not necessary to supply an output file name. UNPACK uses the names, dates, times, and attributes of the original uncompressed files.

UNPACK can copy regular files in addition to packed files, and so can be used to process a disk containing a combination of packed and unpacked files.

VER

 OS/2   DOS

The VER command displays the OS/2 operating system version number.

• **SYNTAX AND DESCRIPTION**

VER

This command is available at both the OS/2 and DOS command prompts, and always displays the OS/2 version number; the DOS version number is never displayed.

• **EXAMPLES**

To display the OS/2 version number, type

VER

VERIFY

The VERIFY command confirms that files written to a disk have been written correctly.

• SYNTAX AND DESCRIPTION

VERIFY *ON*

turns recording verification on, and

VERIFY *OFF*

turns it off again. This is the default setting.

• EXAMPLES

To turn on disk-write verification, type

VERIFY ON

and to suspend disk-write verification, type

VERIFY OFF

Type the command with no parameters to check the current status.

• NOTES   When VERIFY is turned on, you will receive an error message when a write error is detected.

VIEW

The VIEW command displays the contents of online help documents such as the *OS/2 Command Reference*.

• SYNTAX AND DESCRIPTION

VIEW *filename* topic

VIEW displays document files with the file-name extension of .INF, such as CMDREF.INF (Command Reference) or REXX.INF (REXX Information). You do not have to specify the file-name extension of the document file. If you know the name of the topic you are interested in, you can add that name to the command line.

• EXAMPLES

To open the *OS/2 Command Reference* file on the COPY command, type

VIEW C:\OS2\BOOK\CMDREF COPY

To look in the REXX.INF file at the CALL instruction, type

VIEW C:\OS2\BOOK\REXX CALL

• NOTES   See also HELP.

VMDISK

The VMDISK command creates a file that contains the image of a DOS boot disk. You can then use this file to create a DOS session.

• SYNTAX AND DESCRIPTION

VMDISK *sourcedrive:* targetdrive:\path***filename**

In the VMDISK command, *sourcedrive:* specifies the floppy disk drive where the DOS startup disk is located; *targetdrive:* \path\filename represents the image file. You must specify a file name for the image file. Also, the target drive must have more available space than the source drive.

• EXAMPLES

To create an image file of a MS-DOS 5 startup disk in the root directory of drive C, place the startup disk in drive B, and type

VMDISK B: C:\DOS50.IMG

• NOTES See also FSACCESS, FSFILTER.

VOL

The VOL command displays the disk volume label and volume serial number if they exist.

• SYNTAX AND DESCRIPTION

VOL *drive:*

Type this command with no parameters to see information for the current drive.

In a DOS session, you can only see information for one drive at a time. Under OS/2, you can see information on multiple drives.

• EXAMPLES

To display volume label and volume serial number information for the current drive, type

VOL

To see this information for a disk in drive A, type

VOL A:

In an OS/2 session, you can use several drive designations with one VOL command, as follows:

VOL A: B: C:

and see information on all three drives.

• NOTES   See also FORMAT, LABEL.

XCOPY

The XCOPY command copies groups of files or subdirectories.

• SYNTAX AND DESCRIPTION

XCOPY *source destination* /*switches*

In the XCOPY command *source* specifies the file or files to
copy, and may include a directory name, and *target* specifies the
location and name of the copied files. You can use the wildcard
characters * and ? if you wish.

XCOPY is almost always faster than the COPY command when
copying groups of files because of its more efficient use of available
memory.

• SWITCHES

/A	Copies files that have the archive attribute set, but does not change the attribute.
/M	Copies files that have the archive attribute set, but turns off the archive attribute. You can use the ATTRIB command to reset this attribute if you wish.
/D:*mm-dd-yy*	Copies files created or changed on or after the specified date.
/P	Prompts you before copying each file.
/S	Copies directories and subdirectories; does not copy empty subdirectories.
/E	Copies directories and subdirectories, even empty subdirectories.
/V	Performs a verification check to make sure that the data has been written to disk correctly.
/F	Halts the XCOPY operation if the destination file system does not support HPFS extended attributes.

• EXAMPLES

To copy all the files in the current directory to a floppy disk in drive
B, type

XCOPY *.* B:

To duplicate the entire directory structure of drive A onto drive C, type

XCOPY A:\ C:\ /S /E

● **NOTES** XCOPY does not copy hidden or system files.

See also ATTRIB, BACKUP, COPY, RESTORE, VERIFY.

Part VI

CONFIG.SYS Commands

The CONFIG.SYS file is a text file containing system configuration commands which are loaded each time you start your computer. In OS/2, the CONFIG.SYS file is likely to contain 60 or 70 lines of entries, unlike the MS-DOS 5 version of CONFIG.SYS, which might contain 5 to 10 lines at most.

You can use the OS/2 Enhanced Editor to look at or change the contents of CONFIG.SYS, but remember that any changes you make to the file will take effect only after you restart your computer.

This section lists all the configuration commands you can use in CONFIG.SYS, with command descriptions, syntax, and examples.

AUTOFAIL

The AUTOFAIL command specifies how certain error information will be displayed.

• SYNTAX AND DESCRIPTION

AUTOFAIL = *state*

The AUTOFAIL command *state* can be set to NO, in which case a window will open to inform you about hard system errors, or to YES, in which case you will just see an error code. Hard system errors are errors that may require the system to be reconfigured before the operating system can run correctly.

• EXAMPLES

To make OS/2 display an error number when a hard error is encountered, add the following to your CONFIG.SYS file and reboot your computer:

AUTOFAIL = YES

If you want to see a window appear instead, use:

AUTOFAIL = NO

• NOTES   The default setting is AUTOFAIL = NO.

BASEDEV

The BASEDEV command installs a base device driver by specifying the complete file name of the device driver in CONFIG.SYS.

• SYNTAX AND DESCRIPTION

BASEDEV *filename* arguments

where *filename* specifies the name and extension of the device driver file, and *arguments* specifies any additional information needed by the device driver.

A device driver is a file that contains special code needed by the operating system to work with a specific piece of hardware. Device drivers are loaded only as needed, thus relieving the operating system of having to know about all possible hardware options. Base device drivers are needed when OS/2 is first started, and include support for hard and floppy disks, printers, and other devices. Installable device drivers are handled by the DEVICE command described later in this section.

The following list describes some of the commonly used base device drivers included with OS/2:

PRINT01.SYS	Supports local printers on non-Micro Channel computers.
PRINT02.SYS	Supports local printers on Micro Channel computers.
IBM1FLPY.ADD	Supports floppy disk drives on non-Micro Channel computers.
IBM2FLPY.ADD	Supports floppy disk drives on Micro Channel computers.

IBM1S506.ADD	Supports non-SCSI disk drives on non-Micro Channel computers.
IBM2ADSK.ADD	Supports non-SCSI disk drives on Micro Channel computers.
IBM2SCSI.ADD	Supports SCSI disk drives on Micro Channel computers.
IBMINT13.I13	Supports other devices on non-Micro Channel computers.
OS2DASD.DMD	Supports disk drives.
OS2SCSI.DMD	Supports non-disk SCSI devices.

• EXAMPLES

A typical non-Micro Channel computer might have the following statements in CONFIG.SYS:

BASEDEV = PRINT01.SYS
BASEDEV = IBM1LFPY.SYS
BASEDEV = IBM1S506.SYS
BASEDEV = OS2DASD.DMD

• **NOTES**   The BASEDEV command cannot contain drive or path information, because BASEDEV statements are processed before OS/2 can establish a path. All base device drivers must be located in either the root directory of the boot disk or in the C:\OS2 directory.

BASEDEV statements are not necessarily processed in the order in which they appear in CONFIG.SYS, but in the following order of file-name extension:

- .SYS
- .BID
- .VSD
- .TSD
- .ADD
- .I13

- .FLT
- .DMD

Files with other file-name extensions will not be loaded.

See also DEVICE.

BREAK

The BREAK command tells DOS to check to see if the Ctrl+Break keys have been pressed.

• SYNTAX AND DESCRIPTION

BREAK = *state*

The *state* parameter can be either ON or OFF. If BREAK = ON, the operating system checks to see if you pressed the Ctrl+Break keys before executing any program requests. If BREAK = OFF, the operating system checks for the Ctrl+Break keys during keyboard and standard operations.

• EXAMPLES

To have OS/2 check for Ctrl+Break before executing any program requests, use

BREAK = ON

• NOTES   If you accepted the default for BREAK during installation, you will find the following statement in your CONFIG.SYS file:

BREAK = OFF

BUFFERS

The BUFFERS command specifies the number of disk buffers available to the system.

• SYNTAX AND DESCRIPTION

BUFFERS = *n*

In the BUFFERS command, n specifies the number of 512-byte buffers allocated when the operating system starts.

A *buffer* is a method of temporary storage for information read from and written to disk. You can increase the speed of your system by increasing the BUFFERS specification in CONFIG.SYS, but as always, this is a trade-off; the more buffers you specify, the less memory available for other uses.

• EXAMPLES

To increase the number of buffers on your system from 30 to 50, add the following statement to your CONFIG.SYS file:

BUFFERS = 50

• **NOTES**   The default setting for BUFFERS is 30, but you can use any number from 1 to 100; numbers higher than 100 are ignored.

CACHE

The CACHE command sets various parameters for HPFS caching, and is available only if you formatted a hard disk partition for use with the HPFS.

• SYNTAX AND DESCRIPTION

CACHE /switches

Type this command with no parameters to see the current setting used for CACHE.

• SWITCHES

/LAZY:*state*   When set to OFF, specifies that data
                           should be written to disk
                           immediately; when set to ON,
                           specifies that data should be written
                           to disk when the disk is idle.

/MAXAGE:*time*   Specifies the length of time, in
                           milliseconds, before data is
                           transferred to another cache level or
                           to disk. The default is 5000.

/DISKIDLE:*time*   Specifies the length of time, in
                           milliseconds, that the disk must be
                           idle before it can receive data from
                           cache memory. The default is 1000,
                           and must be larger than the value
                           specified for /BUFFERIDLE.

/BUFFERIDLE:*time*   Specifies the length of time, in
                           milliseconds, that the cache can be
                           idle before the information is written
                           to disk. The default is 500.

• EXAMPLES

To set the cache so that all cache information is written out to disk immediately, add the following line to your STARTUP.CMD file:

C:\OS2\CACHE.EXE /LAZY:OFF

To make CACHE write data that has been in memory longer than 4000 milliseconds, add this entry to your CONFIG.SYS file:

RUN=C:\OS2\CACHE.EXE /MAXAGE:4000

• **NOTES**   The /LAZY switch is available at the OS/2 command prompt, the other switches are accessible only through settings in CONFIG.SYS. If you reset /LAZY during an OS/2 session and want to change it again without exiting the session, you must first use the DETATCH command, as follows:

DETATCH CACHE /LAZY:ON

If you specify /LAZY:*ON*, always select the Shut Down command from the desktop before turning off your system. If you don't, you may lose data if the contents of the cache buffers are not written out to disk.

See also DETATCH.

CODEPAGE

The CODEPAGE command specifies the system code pages for code-page switching.

• SYNTAX AND DESCRIPTION

CODEPAGE = *ppp*, *sss*

Use *ppp* to specify the number of the primary code page, and *sss* to specify the number of the secondary code page.

You must also include the appropriate DEVINFO statements for keyboard, printer, and video for both pages in your CONFIG.SYS file.

• EXAMPLES

To prepare the U.S. code page and the multilingual code page as the primary and secondary code pages, respectively, add the following line to your CONFIG.SYS file:

CODEPAGE=437, 850

• NOTES   The CHCP command in Part V, "OS/2 Commands,"
contains a list of the code page numbers for both primary and secondary code pages.

See also COUNTRY, DEVINFO.

COUNTRY

The COUNTRY command prepares OS/2 for international use, and specifies date, time, and decimal separators and currency and case conversions.

• SYNTAX AND DESCRIPTION

COUNTRY = *nnn*, *drive:\path\filename*

In the COUNTRY command *nnn* specifies a three-digit country-identification code. This code is usually the same as the international dialing code for the country. The *drive:\path\filename* parameter specifies the file that contains the country information; normally, this is C:\OS2\SYSTEM\COUNTRY.SYS.

Country codes are as follows:

Arabic	785
Asian English	099
Australia	061
Belgium	032
Canada, French-speaking	002
Czechoslovakia	042
Denmark	045
Finland	358
France	033
Germany	049
Hebrew-speaking	972
Hungary	036
Iceland	354
Italy	039
Japan	081
Korea	082
Latin America	003
Netherlands	031
Norway	047
Poland	048
Portugal	351
Republic of China	088
Spain	034
Sweden	046
Switzerland	041

Turkey	090
United Kingdom	044
United States	001
Yugoslavia	038

• EXAMPLES

To establish the U.S. standards for dates, times, currencies, and other settings, add the following line to your CONFIG.SYS file:

COUNTRY = 001, C:\OS2\SYSTEM\COUNTRY.SYS

• NOTES   The country setting is always the same for OS/2 and DOS sessions.

See also DEVINFO.

DEVICE

The DEVICE command installs device drivers to support mice, touch pads, printers, and other hardware.

• GENERAL SYNTAX AND DESCRIPTION

DEVICE = *drive:\path***filename** */switches*

The *drive:\path\filename* parameter specifies the path and file name containing the device driver, while the */switches* vary in usage from device driver to device driver.

The following list describes the most common device drivers supplied with OS/2:

ANSI.SYS	Provides extended screen and keyboard support for DOS sessions.
COM.SYS	Allows OS/2 programs to use serial ports. This device driver does not take any parameters or switches.
EGA.SYS	Supports EGA video adapters for DOS programs. This device driver does not take any parameters or switches.
EXTDSKDD.SYS	Supports external floppy disks.
LOG.SYS	Supports system error logging using the SYSLOG utility.
MOUSE.SYS	Provides mouse support.
PMDD.SYS	Supplies pointer draw support for OS/2 sessions. This device driver does not take any parameters or switches.
POINTDD.SYS	Provides mouse draw pointer support. This device driver does not take any parameters or switches.
TOUCH.SYS	Provides support for touch devices.
VDISK.SYS	Provides virtual disk support.
VEMM.SYS	DOS expanded-memory manager.
VXMS.SYS	DOS extended-memory manager.

• SWITCHES

Different device drivers use different switches. Those device drivers that have no switches are not shown in the following list.

Switches for ANSI.SYS are as follows:

/X   Allows keys with extended key values to be redefined as distinct keys.

/L   Maintains the same number of screen rows specified
            by the MODE command, and ignores the application
            program settings.

/K   Disables extended keyboard support.

Switches for EXTDSKDD.SYS are as follows:

/D:*d*   Specifies the physical drive number, from 0 to 255.

/T:*t*   Specifies the number of tracks per side, from 1 to
            999; the default is 80.

/S:*s*   Specifies the number of sectors per track, from 1 to
            99; the default is 9.

/H:*h*   Specifies the number of disk heads, from 1 to 99; the
            default is 2.

/F:*f*   Specifies the floppy disk drive type, as follows:

            0 = 360K 5.25"

            1 = 1.2MB 5.25"

            2 = 720K 3.5"

            7 = 1.44MB 3.5"

            9 = 2.88MB 3.5"

Switches for LOG.SYS are as follows:

/E:*n*   Specifies the size of the error-log buffer; the
            minimum is 4K, the default is 8K, and the
            maximum is 64K.

/A:*n*   Specifies the size of the entry alert notification
            buffer; the minimum is 4K, there is no default, and
            the maximum is 64K.

/OFF   Disables error logging as soon as the device driver
            is loaded.

Switches for VDISK.SYS are as follows:

bytes   Sets the size of the virtual disk. The minimum
            is 16K, the default is 64K, and the maximum is
            4096K.

sectors	Sets the sector size to 128, 256, 512, or 1024. The default is 128.
directories	Sets the number of directory entries. The minimum is 2, the default is 64, and the maximum is 1024.

Switches for VEMM.SYS are as follows:

n	Limits the amount of expanded memory available to each DOS session. The default is 4MB, and the maximum is 32MB.

Switches for VXMS.SYS are as follows:

/XXMLIMIT = *g,i*	Sets a system-wide memory maximum to *g*K, and the per-DOS session maximum of *i*K. The default values are /XMMLIMIT = 4096, 1024.
/HMAMIN = *d*	Sets the minimum request size for a high memory area request to succeed, from 0K to 63K.
/NUMHANDLES = *n*	Sets the number of handles per DOS session. The minimum is 0, the default 32, and the maximum 128.
/UMB	Creates upper memory blocks.
/NOUMB	Does not create upper memory blocks.

• EXAMPLES

To install a serial mouse on COM1, add these lines to CONFIG.SYS:

```
DEVICE = C:\OS2\POINTDD.SYS
DEVICE = C:\OS2\MOUSE.SYS SERIAL=COM1
```

To create a 1MB virtual disk with 128-byte sectors and up to 1024 directories, use

```
DEVICE = C:\OS2\VDISK.SYS 1024, 128, 1024
```

• **NOTES**   Load COM.SYS last if you are loading several serial port drivers. To configure a mouse, add POINTDD.SYS and MOUSE.SYS statements (in that order) to your CONFIG.SYS file, and both should load before COM.SYS.

See also BASEDEV and DEVICEHIGH in this section, and MODE and SYSLOG in Part V, "OS/2 Commands."

DEVICEHIGH

The DEVICEHIGH command loads a particular DOS device driver into an upper memory block.

• SYNTAX AND DESCRIPTION

DEVICEHIGH *SIZE=xx drive:\path***filename** *arguments*

In the DEVICEHIGH command, the *SIZE=xx* statement establishes the amount of upper memory required by the device driver, *drive:\path\filename* represents the name of the device driver, and *arguments* represents any optional parameters you want to pass to the device driver.

• EXAMPLES

To load the ANSI.SYS device driver into upper memory, add the following line to your CONFIG.SYS file:

DEVICEHIGH = C:\OS2\MDOS\ANSI.SYS

• **NOTES**   If there is insufficient room to load the device driver into upper memory, the operating system loads it into conventional memory instead.

DEVINFO

The DEVINFO command prepares a device for code-page switching.

• SYNTAX AND DESCRIPTION

To prepare a keyboard, use the following syntax:

DEVINFO = **KBD,layout**,*drive:\path***filename**

where *layout* specifies a country code, and *filename* is KEY-BOARD.DCP that translates keystrokes. Country codes are as follows:

BE	Belgium
CF	Canada, French-speaking
CS	Czechoslovakia
DK	Denmark
SU	Finland
FR	France
FR120	France, alternate keyboard
GR	Germany
HU	Hungary
IS	Iceland
IT	Italy
IT142	Italy, alternate keyboard
LA	Latin America
NL	Netherlands
NO	Norway
PL	Poland

PO	Portugal
SP	Spain
SV	Sweden
SF	Switzerland, French-speaking
SG	Switzerland, German-speaking
TR	Turkey
UK	United Kingdom
UK168	United Kingdom, alternate keyboard
US	United States
YU	Yugoslavia

To prepare a display, use the following syntax:

DEVINFO = *SCR,type,drive:\path\filename*

In this variation of the DEVINFO command, *type* describes a reserved device name from the following: CGA, EGA, VGA, or BGA, and *filename* must be VIOTBL.DCP.

To prepare a printer, use the following:

DEVINFO = *LPT#,device*, *drive:\path\filename, ROM=xxx,yyy*

Here *device* specifies the physical device number, 4201 for an IBM Proprinter I or II, and 5202 for an IBM Quietwriter; and *filename* is either 4201.DCP or 5202.DCP. *ROM* specifies that system code pages are contained in ROM, *xxx* represents the code-page number, and *yyy* is the font identification number associated with this code page. See your IBM printer handbook for more information.

• SWITCHES

None.

• EXAMPLES

To prepare a U.S. keyboard, use the following line in CONFIG.SYS:

DEVINFO=KBD,US,C:\OS2\KEYBOARD.DCP

To set a VGA display for a new code page, use the following:

DEVINFO=SCR,VGA,C:\OS2\VIOTBL.DCP

• **NOTES**   See also COUNTRY in this section, and CHCP and KEYB in Part V, "OS/2 Commands."

DISKCACHE

The DISKCACHE command specifies the amount of memory to use for the disk cache and for cache control information.

• SYNTAX AND DESCRIPTION

DISKCACHE = *n*,*LW*,*T*,*AC*:*x*

In the DISKCACHE command, *n* specifies a number from 64 to 14400, which represents the number of 1024-byte blocks used for control information in the disk cache. The default is 64. *T* indicates the threshold size for the number of sectors that will be loaded into the cache, from 4 to 128, with a default of 4. *LW* specifies that the cache contents are written to disk only during disk-idle time; leave this parameter out to make the cache write to disk immediately. The *AC*:*x* autocheck parameter checks the specified startup drive to make sure that the file system is intact.

• EXAMPLES

To set a cache size of 256K, with a threshold size of 32, and information written to disk immediately, use

DISKCACHE=256,32

• NOTES

Recommended disk cache sizes are as follows: systems with 2MB to 3MB of memory should use a cache of 64K, systems with 4MB to 5MB should use a cache of 192K, and systems with more than 6MB should use a cache size of 256K.

DOS

DOS

The DOS command specifies that the DOS operating system will be loaded into the high memory area (HMA), and whether DOS or an application program controls upper memory blocks (UMBs).

• SYNTAX AND DESCRIPTION

DOS = place,blocks

In the DOS command, *place* can be either HIGH to load the operating system kernel into the high memory area, or LOW to load the kernel into conventional memory. The *block* parameter can be set to UMB, in which case the operating system controls the allocation of upper memory blocks, or NOUMB, which means that applications programs can allocate upper memory blocks but cannot be located there.

• EXAMPLES

The OS/2 installation program adds this line to CONFIG.SYS:

DOS=LOW, NOUMB

This means that DOS application programs can allocate UMBs and that the DOS kernel is loaded into conventional memory below 640K.

• NOTES   See also DEVICEHIGH and LOADHIGH.

DPATH

The DPATH command sets a search path for application programs to locate data files outside the current directory. Use the SET command in CONFIG.SYS to specify the DPATH environment variable.

• SYNTAX AND DESCRIPTION

SET DPATH = *drive:\path*

In the DPATH command *drive:\path* specifies the drive or drives and directories to be searched for data files. DPATH is an operating system environment variable, so that application programs can access this information and can act accordingly.

Type the command from the command prompt with no parameters to see a display of the current setting of DPATH, and type **DPATH;** from the prompt to clear the current setting.

• EXAMPLES

To display the current DPATH setting, type the following at the command prompt:

DPATH

To set the DPATH variable in CONFIG.SYS to include the OS2 and SYSTEM directories, add the following line:

SET DPATH = C:\OS2\SYSTEM

• NOTES   See also PATH, SET.

FCBS

The FCBS command establishes file-control block information for DOS sessions.

• SYNTAX AND DESCRIPTION

FCBS = *m,n*

In the FCBS command, *m* represents the number of file-control blocks DOS can open at once, and *n* represents the number of FCBs that DOS cannot close to make room for new FCBs.

• EXAMPLES

To set the number of FCBs to 10, add the following to your CON-FIG.SYS file:

FCBS = 10

FILES

The FILES command establishes the number of files that can be open in a DOS session. This command has no effect on an OS/2 session.

• SYNTAX AND DESCRIPTION

FILES = *n*

In the FILES command, *n* establishes the number of files that can be open at the same time, from 20 to 255. The default value, set when OS/2 is installed, is 20.

• EXAMPLES

To specify 20 as the number of files that DOS can open in a session at any time, add the following line to your CONFIG.SYS file:

FILES = 20

IFS

The IFS command installs a file system by specifying the drive, path, and file name of the file system program.

• SYNTAX AND DESCRIPTION

IFS = *drive:\path**filename** /switches*

• SWITCHES

/CACHE:*nnn*	Specifies the amount of memory for file system disk caching.
/AUTOCHECK:*nnn*	Specifies the drive letter you want to check at system startup to determine if the file system is in an inconsistent state.
/CRECL:*x*	Specifies the maximum record size for caching. The minimum is 2K, the default is 4K, and the maximum is 64K.

• EXAMPLES

The OS/2 installation program adds the following line to your CONFIG.SYS file:

IFS = C:\OS2\HPFS.IFS /CACHE:64 /CRECL:4

IOPL

The IOPL command specifies whether any OS/2 processes can issue direct input/output statements.

• SYNTAX AND DESCRIPTION

IOPL = *state*

In the IOPL command, *state* can be set to NO, to prevent direct input/output statements; to YES, to allow direct input/output statements; or to *list*, which restricts the privilege to those programs named in the list.

• EXAMPLES

To allow processes to make direct input/output instructions, add the following line to your CONFIG.SYS file:

IOPL = YES

LASTDRIVE

The LASTDRIVE command establishes the maximum number of drives for a DOS session.

• SYNTAX AND DESCRIPTION

LASTDR*IVE* = *x*

The *x* parameter specifies a drive letter, from A to Z, and must reflect the minimum number of physical drives you have installed on your system.

• SWITCHES

None.

• EXAMPLES

To establish drive N as the 14th drive on your system, add the following line to your CONFIG.SYS file:

LASTDRIVE = N

LH OR LOADHIGH

The LH command loads terminate-and-stay resident (TSR) programs into upper memory blocks (UMB) if they are available.

LH is an abbreviation for LOADHIGH; you can use either as they both do the same thing.

• SYNTAX AND DESCRIPTION

LH *drive:\path**filename** arguments*

The *drive:\path\filename* specifies the drive, directory, and file name for the TSR, and *arguments* adds any additional parameters needed for the TSR. If upper memory blocks are not available DOS will automatically load the TSR into conventional memory.

• EXAMPLES

To load the TSR program TOOL into a UMB, add the following to your CONFIG.SYS file:

DOS = UMB

Then add the following line to your AUTOEXEC.BAT file:

LH C:\MYSTUFF\TOOL

• NOTES   See also DEVICEHIGH, DOS.

LIBPATH

The LIBPATH command establishes a path to identify the location of dynamic link libraries (DLL).

• SYNTAX AND DESCRIPTION

LIBPATH = *drive:**path***

The *drive:\path* parameter establishes the path information for LIB-PATH. This setting is not part of the operating system environment information.

• EXAMPLES

When you install OS/2, the installation program adds a line similar to the following to your CONFIG.SYS file:

LIBPATH = C:\OS2\DLL;C:\OS2\MDOS;C:\OS2\APPS\DLL;

MAXWAIT

OS/2

The MAXWAIT command establishes the length of time that a process must wait before the system assigns a higher priority.

• SYNTAX AND DESCRIPTION

MAXWAIT = *x*

The *x* parameter is the number of seconds, from 1 to 255, that must elapse before the priority is increased.

• EXAMPLES

To make a process wait for 3 seconds (the default setting) before receiving an increase in priority, add the following line to your CONFIG.SYS file:

MAXWAIT = 3

MEMMAN

The MEMMAN command controls OS/2's use of virtual memory.

• SYNTAX AND DESCRIPTION

MEMMAN = *parameters*

There are four groups of parameters you can use with this command. The first group has two states, SWAP or NOSWAP. SWAP allows segment swapping and storage compaction, and NOSWAP prevents it.

The second group also has two options, MOVE and NOMOVE. These options are provided for OS/2 1.3 compatibility. The third setting, COMMIT, is new in OS/2 version 2.1; it forces OS/2 to reserve space in the swap file.

Finally, PROTECT, enables certain APIs to allocate and use protected memory.

• EXAMPLES

To support virtual memory swapping and to give APIs access to protected memory, add the following line into your CONFIG.SYS file:

MEMMAN = SWAP,PROTECT

• NOTES   See also SWAPPATH.

PATH

| OS/2 | | DOS |

The PATH command sets a search path for application programs to locate program files outside the current directory. Use the SET command in CONFIG.SYS to specify the PATH environment variable.

• SYNTAX AND DESCRIPTION

SET PATH = *drive:\path*

In the PATH command *drive:\path* specifies the drive or drives and directories to be searched for program files. PATH is an operating system environment variable, so that application programs can access this information and can act accordingly.

You can also use the PATH from the command prompt:

PATH = *drive\path*

Use the command with no parameters to see a display of the current setting of PATH, and type **PATH;** from the prompt to clear the current setting.

• EXAMPLES

To set the path to include the OS/2 directory, add the following PATH statement into your CONFIG.SYS file:

SET PATH = C:\OS2

• **NOTES**   The PATH command locates only executable files; in a DOS session, this includes files with the file-name extensions of .COM, .BAT, or .EXE. In an OS/2 session PATH also works with the .CMD file-name extension.

See also DPATH, SET.

PAUSEONERROR

The PAUSEONERROR command establishes whether CONFIG.SYS pauses or continues when it encounters an error.

• SYNTAX AND DESCRIPTION

PAUSEONERRO*R* = *state*

The *state* parameter can be either YES, in which case the system pauses, or NO, when it doesn't.

• EXAMPLES

To prevent the system from pausing if it encounters an error during CONFIG.SYS processing, add the following line to your CONFIG.SYS file:

PAUSEONERROR = NO

• NOTES   If there is no PAUSEONERROR statement in CONFIG.SYS, the operating system interprets that as PAUSEONERROR = YES.

PRINTMONBUFSIZE

The PRINTMONBUFSIZE command establishes the size of the parallel port device driver buffer.

• SYNTAX AND DESCRIPTION

PRINTMONBUFSIZE = *x, y, z*

In this command, the x, y, and z parameters establish the size of the buffers for LPT1, LPT2, and LPT3, respectively. The minimum value is 134 bytes and the maximum is 2048 bytes.

• EXAMPLES

The OS/2 Installation program sets up these buffers with the default size of 134 bytes with the following line in CONFIG.SYS:

PRINTMONBUFSIZE 134,134,134

PRIORITY

The PRIORITY command establishes the priority level for all threads.

• SYNTAX AND DESCRIPTION

PRIORITY = *state*

The *state* parameter can be set to DYNAMIC or to ABSOLUTE. DYNAMIC, the default setting, establishes a priority dependent on the availability of system resources, while ABSOLUTE sets a rigid priority system.

• EXAMPLES

To ensure OS/2 always maintains the priority of a thread, and never changes it even when system load changes, add the following line to your CONFIG.SYS file:

PRIORITY = ABSOLUTE

• NOTES   See also MAXWAIT, TIMESLICE, and THREADS.

PRIORITY_DISK_IO

The PRIORITY_DISK_IO command establishes disk priority for foreground applications.

• SYNTAX AND DESCRIPTION

PRIORITY_DISK_IO = *state*

state can be either YES or NO. YES establishes that foreground applications have priority over background processes. This is the default state. A setting of NO specifies that all applications have the same priority, and are treated equally with respect to disk access.

• EXAMPLES

To specify that foreground applications should have priority over background applications, use the following line in CONFIG.SYS:

PRIORITY_DISK_IO = YES

PROTECTONLY

The PROTECTONLY command allows you to choose between operating environments.

• SYNTAX AND DESCRIPTION

PROTECTONLY = *state*

In this command, *state* can be set to either YES or NO. When set to NO, this option selects both OS/2 and DOS environments. This is the default. When set to YES, it selects OS/2 sessions only.

• EXAMPLES

To select both OS/2 and DOS sessions, add the following line to CONFIG.SYS:

PROTECTONLY = NO

• NOTES   See also PROTSHELL, RMSIZE, SHELL.

PROTSHELL

The PROTSHELL command loads the OS/2 user interface and command processor. PROTSHELL can also replace the default command processor with another command processor.

• SYNTAX AND DESCRIPTION

PROTSHELL *drive:\path**filename*** *arguments*

The *drive:\path\filename* parameter specifies the name of the existing or replacement command processor file, and *arguments* represents any additional options needed for the command processor.

• EXAMPLES

The standard OS/2 user interface requires several configuration statements in CONFIG.SYS, as follows:

PROTSHELL=C:\OS2\PMSHELL.EXE
SET USER_INI=C:\OS2\OS2.INI
SET SYSTEM_INI=C:\OS2\OS2SYS.INI
SET OS2_SHELL=C:\OS2\CMD.EXE
SET AUTOSTART=PROGRAMS,TASKLIST,FOLDERS

To establish your own file, MYFACE.EXE, as the user interface, change the first of these lines as shown, then delete the SET AUTOSTART line above to disable the OS/2 workplace shell.

PROTSHELL=C:\OS2\MYFACE.EXE
SET USER_INI=C:\OS2\OS2.INI
SET SYSTEM_INI=C:\OS2\OS2SYS.INI
SET OS2_SHELL=C:\OS2\CMD.EXE

• NOTES   See also PROTECTONLY, RMSIZE, and SHELL.

RMSIZE

DOS

The RMSIZE command tells a DOS session how much memory is available.

• SYNTAX AND DESCRIPTION

RMSIZE = *xxx*

In the RMSIZE command, the *xxx* parameter represents the amount of memory available to the DOS session, from 0 to 640, where each number is equivalent to 1024 bytes or 1K. If you specify a number greater than 640K, or greater than the total amount of physical memory available if it is less than 640K, then the operating system ignores this command and calculates its own default value.

• EXAMPLES

To limit the size of the DOS session to 512K, add the following line to your CONFIG.SYS file:

RMSIZE = 512

• NOTES   See also PROTECTONLY, PROTSHELL, SHELL.

RUN

The RUN command starts an OS/2 system program running in the background when the system starts. The RUN command does not start OS/2 application programs.

• SYNTAX AND DESCRIPTION

RUN = *drive:\path***filename** */switches*

The *drive:\path\filename* parameter specifies the name of the system program you want to run. For example, the OS/2 utility LOG-DAEM.EXE monitors and records system errors. The */switches* parameter adds any optional switches needed by this program.

• SWITCHES

If you run LOGDAEM.EXE, you can use the switches listed below. No other system programs that work with RUN take switches.

/E:*filename*	Specifies the name of the error-log file. This file is created in C:\OS2\SYSTEM unless you specify otherwise.
/W:*n*	Sets the size of the error-log file, from a minimum of 4K. The default is 64K.

• EXAMPLES

To run LOGDAEM.EXE using the default file name and a file size of 128K, add the following line to your CONFIG.SYS file:

RUN=C:\OS2\SYSTEM\LOGDAEM.EXE /W:128

To load and start the program LVIS.EXE from the C:\STUFF directory, add this line to your CONFIG.SYS file:

RUN=C:\STUFF\LVIS.EXE

• **NOTES**   See also DEVICE in this section, and SYSLOG in Part V, "OS/2 Commands."

The SET command specifies, changes, or deletes environment variables. You can use the SET command from the command prompt, but its most common use is to establish environment variables from CONFIG.SYS when the system starts.

• **SYNTAX AND DESCRIPTION**

SET *string1 = string2*

The environment variables control the way that a session works. These variables are available to all application programs, and specify information including the PATH and DPATH settings as well as aspects of the user interface.

Type the SET command without a parameter to see a list of the current environment settings on the screen.

To establish an environment variable, *string1* is the variable you want to set, and *string2* is the value you want to assign to *string1*. If a value already exists for the variable, a second SET command will overwrite the original value with the new value. If you use SET with just *string1* and the equals sign, the command processor removes the environment variable name and associated value from the environment.

• EXAMPLES

To display the present environment variables, type

SET

Add the following statement to CONFIG.SYS to set the default OS/2 prompt:

SET PROMPT = $i[$p]

• NOTES See also DPATH, PATH, PROMPT.

SHELL

The SHELL command loads and starts the DOS command processor, COMMAND.COM, or lets you replace the default command processor with your own.

• SYNTAX AND DESCRIPTION

SHELL = *drive:\path***filename** *arguments*

In the SHELL command, the *drive:\path\filename* parameter defines the file that contains the command processor. The default is COMMAND.COM, but you can use your own if you wish. The *arguments* parameter sets any optional switches for this command processor.

• SWITCHES

If you use COMMAND.COM, you can use the following switch:

/P   Keeps the command processor in memory.

• EXAMPLES

To load the DOS command processor, COMMAND.COM, and keep it in memory until the computer is shut down, add the following line to your CONFIG.SYS file:

SHELL=C:\OS2\MDOS\COMMAND.COM C:\OS2\MDOS /P

• NOTES   See also COMMAND, PROTSHELL, RMSIZE.

SWAPPATH

The SWAPPATH command specifies the size and location of the virtual memory swap file.

• SYNTAX AND DESCRIPTION

SWAPPATH = *drive:**path minfree*

The *drive:\path* parameter specifies the location of the swap file, SWAPPER.DAT, and *minfree* specifies the minimum amount of space you want to have free on the drive after the creation of the swap file. This means that the swap file can only grow to a size that leaves this amount of space free on the drive. *minfree* is specified in K, and can be any size, from 512K to 32767K.

• EXAMPLES

To create a swap file that leaves at least 2048K of disk space free, add the following line to your CONFIG.SYS file:

SWAPPATH=C:\OS2\SYSTEM 2048

• **NOTES**   For swapping to take place, you must also have the following command in CONFIG.SYS:

MEMMAN = SWAP

See also MEMMAN.

THREADS

The THREADS command specifies the maximum number of threads an OS/2 session can create at one time.

• SYNTAX AND DESCRIPTION

THREADS = *xxx*

In OS/2, more than one thread can exist at the same time inside a single process or application program. The *xxx* parameter specifies the maximum number of threads that can exist in an OS/2 session, from 32 to 4095; the default is 64.

• EXAMPLES

To establish the maximum number of threads that can run at the same time in an OS/2 session as 256, add the following to your CONFIG.SYS file:

THREADS = 256

• **NOTES**   See also MAXWAIT, PRIORITY, TIMESLICE.

TIMESLICE

OS/2

The TIMESLICE command establishes the minimum and maximum amount of processor time allocated to threads and programs in both OS/2 and DOS sessions.

• SYNTAX AND DESCRIPTION

TIMESLICE = *x*, *y*

The x parameter establishes the minimum time, in milliseconds. This value must be a whole number greater than or equal to 32. The y parameter is optional and specifies the maximum time, also in milliseconds. The y value must be greater than or equal to the y value, and less than 65536.

• EXAMPLES

To set the minimum timeslice to 50 milliseconds and the maximum timeslice to 100 milliseconds, add the following line to your CONFIG.SYS file:

TIMESLICE = 50,100

• NOTES   See also MAXWAIT, PRIORITY, THREADS.

TRACE

OS/2

The TRACE command enables or disables tracing of system events. This command is an advanced command intended for use with technical coordinators and technical support staff only.

TRACEBUF

OS/2

The TRACEBUF command sets the size of the trace buffer. This command is an advanced command intended for use with technical coordinators and technical support staff only.

TRACEFMT

OS/2

The TRACEFMT command displays formatted trace records in reverse order of timestamp. This command is an advanced command intended for use with technical coordinators and technical support staff only.

Part VII

Batch File Commands

This section lists alphabetically all the commands you can use in your batch file. Each entry includes a command description, syntax and description, examples, and notes. This section uses the same OS/2 and DOS icons displayed in Part V, "OS/2 Commands."

A *batch file* is just an ASCII text file containing a list of commands. Each line in the batch file contains one command, along with any switches that might be required, in just the same form that you would use at the command line. Batch files can automate complex or little-used commands and can make life much easier.

Use the Enhanced Editor to create your batch file in an OS/2 session or use the EDIT program in a MS-DOS 5 session. You can use any name you like for your batch file, but the file-name extension for an OS/2 session batch file must be .CMD, and the file-name extension for a DOS session batch file must be .BAT.

When you type the name of the batch file at the command prompt, the operating system opens the file and executes the commands that it finds just as if you had typed them from the keyboard.

OS/2 also includes the Restructured Extended Executor (REXX) programming language, which is similar to the batch language but is a full-fledged programming language. Any description of REXX is beyond the scope of this book.

Used at the beginning of a batch file line, @ suppresses the display of the commands that follow.

• SYNTAX AND DESCRIPTION

@command

Command lines that include the @ symbol are processed normally, but are not displayed. The @ symbol must be the first character on the line.

• EXAMPLES

To turn off the display from the ECHO command, add the following line to your batch file:

@ECHO OFF

• NOTES   See also ECHO, REM.

CALL

The CALL command invokes a second batch file from within the current batch file, without ending the first one.

• SYNTAX AND DESCRIPTION

CALL *batchfile* argument

In the CALL command, *batchfile* is the name of the batch file you
want to invoke, including drive and path information as needed,
and *argument* is any specific information you want to pass to this
second batch file.

The second batch file executes, and when it completes, control
returns to the line in the original batch file immediately after the
line that contained the CALL command.

• EXAMPLES

To call a batch file called ADDRESS.CMD, add the following to
your batch file:

CALL ADDRESS

• **NOTES**   In an OS/2 session a batch file may not call itself.
However, this is allowed in a DOS session; just make sure that the
batch file ends itself eventually.

Do not use piping or any kind of redirection with CALL.

ECHO

The ECHO command tells the operating system whether to display
batch commands as they run. You can also use ECHO to display a
text message on the screen.

• SYNTAX AND DESCRIPTION

ECHO *state message*

where *state* can be set to ON or OFF. ECHO ON is the default setting, and displays all commands as they run. ECHO OFF suppresses the display of commands, including the REM command. *message* can be any text, and is displayed regardless of the current setting of *state*.

• EXAMPLES

To display all the commands in a batch file as they are processed, add the following to the beginning of your batch file:

ECHO ON

To turn this output off, use the following instead:

ECHO OFF

• NOTES   See also PAUSE, REM.

ENDLOCAL

The ENDLOCAL command restores the drive, directory, and environment variables to their original condition before the SET-LOCAL command was invoked.

• SYNTAX AND DESCRIPTION

ENDLOCAL

Sometimes it is convenient to use different environment variables during the execution of a particular batch file. Use the SETLOCAL command at the beginning of the batch file to record the current setting of these important system variables. At the end of the batch file use ENDLOCAL to restore these original values back to the environment again. In this way, a batch file can run with its own environment variables without impacting the rest of the system.

• EXAMPLES

When using the SETLOCAL ENDLOCAL pair of commands, be sure to place them before and after any environment variables are changed, as shown in the following example:

SETLOCAL
A:
PATH A:\;A:\ELVIS
CD\ELVIS
ROCKSTAR
ENDLOCAL

In this example, the SETLOCAL command saves the current settings for drive, current directory, path, and other information. Then the batch file makes drive A the current drive, \ELVIS the current directory, and starts the program called ROCKSTAR. When this program finishes, the ENDLOCAL command restores the original drive, directory, and path information back to the environment.

• NOTES   See also SETLOCAL.

EXTPROC

The EXTPROC command specifies that an external batch processor should be used to process a batch file, rather than the usual batch processor.

• SYNTAX AND DESCRIPTION

EXTPROC *filename* arguments

If you ever want to replace the OS/2 batch processor with your own, you can do so using the EXTPROC command. The *filename* parameter specifies the name of the batch processor you want to use, and *arguments* details any extra information you want to pass to the batch processor.

• EXAMPLES

To use the batch processor called MYPROC.EXE located in the MYFILES directory, add the following to your batch file:

EXTPROC C:\MYFILES\MYPROC.EXE

• **NOTES**   The EXTPROC command *must* be the first command in the batch file, because it is still processed by the regular command processor; only the commands that follow will be processed by your batch processor.

FOR

The FOR command allows for the repetitive running of OS/2 commands.

• SYNTAX AND DESCRIPTION

FOR *%%variable* IN *(set)* DO *command*

The FOR command creates a loop in a batch file that allows a single command to repeat on a series of file parameters, until all the parameters are exhausted. In the syntax above, *%%variable* is a symbol to be applied to each item in the *set*, and *command* is the OS/2 command you want to execute repeatedly.

Always enclose *set* in parentheses, and if *set* includes file names, you can use the wildcard characters * and ? if you wish.

• EXAMPLES

To delete all the files in the C:\WRITE directory with the file-name extension of .BAK, add this to your batch file:

FOR %%Y IN (*.BAK) DO DEL C:\WRITE\%%Y

• **NOTES**   You can also invoke the FOR command from the command prompt. In this case, just use one percent sign in the variable symbol, rather than two.

Piping and redirection are available with the FOR command only in OS/2 sessions, not in DOS sessions.

GOTO

The GOTO command transfers batch-file control to a line beginning with a label rather than executing the next command in the file.

• SYNTAX AND DESCRIPTION

GOTO :*label*

The GOTO command sends a batch program to a :*label*, a unique string of up to 8 significant characters on a line by itself, preceded by a colon, where processing continues.

GOTO is often used with IF or IF NOT so that the batch file can respond differently under different circumstances.

• EXAMPLES

When the operating system encounters the statement

GOTO :END

in a batch file, it jumps to the line

:END

where batch file processing continues.

• NOTES   If you try to GOTO a label that does not exist, OS/2 stops processing the batch file and posts an error message. If you use a label without a GOTO, OS/2 ignores the label and continues processing.

See also IF.

IF

 OS/2   DOS

The IF command allows for the conditional processing of batch file commands.

• SYNTAX AND DESCRIPTION

There are several ways to use the IF command to evaluate an error level, a string, or a file name:

IF *ERRORLEVEL n command*

This statement checks the status of *ERRORLEVEL n,* and is true if the previous program had an exit code of *n* or higher. When this is true, the *command* is executed; otherwise the *command* is ignored.

IF *string1==string2 command*

In this syntax, if the two strings are equal, the *command* is executed; otherwise the *command* is ignored. This comparison is case sensitive, so upper- and lowercase must match. The strings must not be blank.

IF *EXIST* drive:\path*filename command*

In this syntax, if the *drive:\path\filename* exists, *command* is executed; if not, *command* is ignored. You can use the wildcard characters * and ? in the file name if you wish.

All of these syntaxes can be reversed by the inclusion of a NOT statement after the IF. For example, the first syntax shown above becomes

IF NOT *ERRORLEVEL n command*

• EXAMPLES

To test an ERRORLEVEL and then branch to a label based on that ERRORLEVEL value, add the following lines to your batch file:

```
IF ERRORLEVEL 4 GOTO FOUR
IF ERRORLEVEL 3 GOTO THREE
IF ERRORLEVEL 2 GOTO TWO
IF ERRORLEVEL 1 GOTO ONE


:FOUR
ECHO NUMBER FOUR
GOTO END
:THREE
ECHO NUMBER THREE
GOTO END
:TWO
ECHO NUMBER TWO
GOTO END
```

```
:ONE
ECHO ONE
GOTO END

:END
```

- **NOTES** See also GOTO.

PAUSE

The PAUSE command suspends batch-file processing and displays the message

Press any key when ready . . .

• SYNTAX AND DESCRIPTION

PAUSE *message*

You can use a *message* with the PAUSE command; it will be displayed only when ECHO is on.

• EXAMPLES

To pause your batch file and display the message "Please change disks," add the following to your batch file:

PAUSE Please change disks

- **NOTES** See also ECHO, REM.

REM

The REM command adds comments to a batch file or to your CONFIG.SYS file.

• SYNTAX AND DESCRIPTION

REM *comments*

Use the REM command to annotate your batch files and your CONFIG.SYS file. After all, a sequence of commands may be obvious to you now, but will that still be true a year from now? The nonexecuting *comments* can be any characters up to a maximum of 123, and they are displayed if ECHO is on. If ECHO is OFF they are not displayed.

You can also temporarily disable a complex entry in your CONFIG.SYS file if you place a REM statement in front of it. This avoids having to delete the entry, and possibly having to rebuild it later.

• EXAMPLES

To display the title "This is a Batch File," add the following to your batch file:

REM This is a Batch File

To suppress this output, use

@REM This is a Batch File

To add three blank lines to a batch file to make it easier to read, add these lines:

REM

REM

REM

• NOTES   See also @, ECHO.

SETLOCAL

The SETLOCAL command saves the current drive, directory, and environment variables, and lets the batch file establish its own variables. The original settings are restored by an ENDLOCAL command, or when the batch file ends.

• SYNTAX AND DESCRIPTION

SETLOCAL

Sometimes it is convenient to use different environment variables during the execution of a particular batch file. Use the SETLOCAL command at the beginning of the batch file to record the current setting of these important system variables. At the end of the batch file use ENDLOCAL to restore these original values back to the environment again. In this way, a batch file can run with its own environment variables without impacting the rest of the system.

• EXAMPLES

When using the SETLOCAL ENDLOCAL pair of commands, be sure to place them before and after any environment variables are changed, as shown in the following example:

SETLOCAL
A:
PATH A:\;A:\ELVIS
CD\ELVIS
ROCKSTAR
ENDLOCAL

In this example, the SETLOCAL command saves the current settings for drive, current directory, path, and other information. Then the batch file makes drive A the current drive, \ELVIS the current directory, and starts the program called ROCKSTAR. When this program finishes, the ENDLOCAL command restores the original drive, directory, and path information back to the environment.

• **NOTES**   See also ENDLOCAL.

The SHIFT command allows you to use more than 10 replaceable parameters in a batch file.

• **SYNTAX AND DESCRIPTION**

SHIFT

Batch files can handle up to 10 replaceable parameters, %0 through %9. If you use the SHIFT command, all parameters on the command line are moved one place to the left; the %1 parameter replaces the %0 parameter, %2 replaces %1, and so on. A new parameter is loaded into %9.

There is no reverse shift command, so after a SHIFT command, the original contents of %0 cannot be recovered.

• **EXAMPLES**

If %0 contains "fat," %1 contains "thin," %2 contains "beards," and %3 through %9 are empty, a SHIFT command produces the following:

%0   thin

%1   beards

and fat is lost.

Index

Page numbers in **boldface** indicate primary references to a topic. Page numbers in *italic* indicate figure references.

Help Yourself with
Another Quality Sybex Book

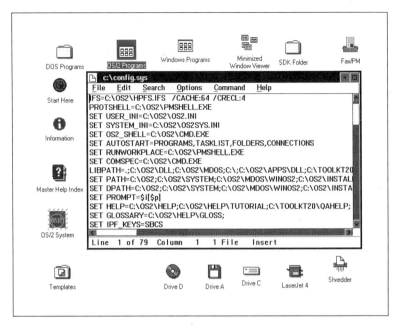

The screen image above shows a window open on the OS/2 desktop, and the table below lists all the keyboard shortcuts you can use when working with windows.

Key	Function
Alt+Spacebar	Opens the pop-up menu for a window
Alt+F4	Closes a window
Alt+F7	Lets you move a window using the arrow keys
Alt+F8	Lets you size a window using the arrow keys
Alt+F9	Minimizes a window
Alt+F10	Maximizes a window
Alt+F11	Hides a window
PgUp, PgDn	Moves through the contents of a window one page at a time